9million:

From Privilege to Prison

PIERS RAVENHILL

Text Piers Ravenhill
Copyright © Piers Ravenhill

First print August 2024

9million:

From Privilege to Prison

To be decided

CONTENTS

CHAPTER 1: A LIFE-CHANGING DRUG BUST — 11

CHAPTER 2: POSH BOY, COMMON BOY — 19

CHAPTER 3: EARLY HUSTLES AND DISCOVERING MY CRIMINAL SIDE — 35

CHAPTER 4: EXPANDING MY CRIMINAL ENTERPRISES — 43

CHAPTER 5: PLAYING WITH FIRE — 51

CHAPTER 6: NCS — 57

CHAPTER 7: THE STENCH OF REALITY — 63

CHAPTER 8: YOU CAN RUN BUT... — 67

CHAPTER 9: WHAT MORE CAN I LOSE...? — 73

CHAPTER 10: SENTENCING - THE NUMBERS GAME — 95

CHAPTER 11: AS ONE DOOR CLOSES... — 105

CHAPTER 12: MAKING THE BEST OF IT	111
CHAPTER 13: LOSING AND LISTENING	115
CHAPTER 14: MAIDSTONE	121
CHAPTER 15: NO POINT IN WASTING OUR TIME...	129
CHAPTER 16: OPEN PRISON CLOSED PRISON	135
CHAPTER 17: KNIFE POINT!	141
CHAPTER 18: OUT OF THE FRYING PAN...	145
THANK YOU	149

CHAPTER 1: A LIFE-CHANGING DRUG BUST

The spring day had started out peacefully enough. As I drove to a run-of-the-mill warehouse in the depths of Surrey to make a large drug deal, I had no idea my world was about to come crashing down around me. The deal should have been straightforward—a simple exchange of 200,000 ecstasy tablets for 250 kg of hashish. I'd done lots of similar deals before with no problems, but little did I know that this meeting on an anonymous industrial estate had been carefully orchestrated by undercover National Crime Squad (NCS) coppers, and I was heading straight into a trap.

I'd built my drug business over the previous decade by reinvesting profits and quietly establishing trusted connections at the top end of the 'game.' By the age of 30, I had stashed away almost £3 million in cash and assets from my illegal dealings, and I had a float of around another million. No one in my life outside of the business had a clue about my various criminal activities. To the casual observer, I was just a personal trainer and small-business owner—I was co-owner of www.sensibleseeds.com—living a relatively quiet life in the suburbs. But, behind closed doors, I was top dog in a sophisticated operation distributing all manner of drug parcels across the south of England and sometimes further afield. I was involved in other criminal activities as well, but drugs were my biggest source of income.

Things were going well that year. Business was flourishing, money was rolling in. In some ways, I felt as though the world was my oyster. My confidence had grown to the point where I never really considered the idea that the glory days might suddenly vanish. In my head, I was about to quietly pull off another big deal without a hitch. But the intricate trap set by NCS was about to snap shut and show me I wasn't as bulletproof as I'd thought.

I had first heard about the potential deal from Ben, a good friend and mid-level drug business associate of mine. We knew each other from local nights out with mutual friends and I also trained in his gym. I didn't know it at the time, but for a while, he had been under surveillance by police who suspected his involvement in drug dealing and fencing stolen goods. Two men, Steve and Kevin, had become members of the gym. They trained regularly and before long they became friendly with Ben, slowly gaining his trust. Things progressed to the point where they were paying cash upfront for increasingly large amounts of drugs—sometimes nine ounces of coke, sometimes 5,000 Es. None of this was known to me—I supplied Ben and what happened after that was not my concern. Apart from the fact that I was managing his finances for him (he had plenty of customers but was shit with money), we didn't interact much at that point. Then one day he called me to say he'd been asked if he knew anyone who could get Steve 200,000 ecstasy tablets—'pills' as we called them. They wanted to trade them for their 250 kg of Moroccan hash —'soap bar' to people in the know.

I agreed to a sit-down, mostly to get a look at these guys. We met at a bog-standard Tesco store café for a brief chat, weighing each other up over meaningless small talk. Steve and I chatted alone, while Kevin and Ben laughed and joked with each other at the other end of the café. Steve was tall, overweight and spoke with a confident air. Kevin—Scottish and clearly ex-military—was, I concluded, the muscle. Steve laid out the idea again as he had already done to Ben, telling me the 'top-notch' soap was sitting in Spain awaiting transfer to the UK. I told him I'd be waiting on him because I knew I could send for 200,000 Es that day if I needed to. That amount didn't phase me in the least. I was used to this kind of deal and had been for years. There was something, though, something I couldn't quite put my finger on, about Steve and Kevin. My street smarts were pretty sharp, so I decided to follow up on what my gut was telling me.

In the car after the meeting, I grilled Ben for more details about these blokes who Steve had self-titled 'the firm' as we sat in that café. He explained they trained regularly at the gym and had bought quantities of drugs on numerous occasions, plus one of the stolen cars I'd also been cloning and selling. They were always on time, collected their goods with no fuss and were always spot-on with their cash payments. According to Ben, they were looking to offload their hash because they never actually wanted it. They were taking it to wipe a debt that had been owed to them for such a long time that they felt it was now the only way to claw back what was due. They didn't deal in hash, it wasn't their thing, but they did deal in Ecstasy—hence the trade they were asking for. I trusted Ben but there was still a slight nagging doubt inside of me. This feeling, coupled with some local whispers saying there was some kind of police operation going on, possibly a drug operation, I have to admit I decided to ignore.

One of the rumours claimed Ben's gym was being bugged by the police. When Ben told me what was being said, I told him to forget it and said he was nowhere near big enough a fish to warrant that kind of scrutiny. I thought about it all for a while and eventually decided the deal, potentially very lucrative for me, would go ahead. I didn't want to bin a good earner on a vague hunch or the mutterings of a few low-level burglars and drug users.

Ben vouching for Steve and Kevin played its part, and I finally gave the deal the thumbs-up. We agreed they would take their soap bar to a secure place where I would check its quality before agreeing to the swap. After several weeks, the hash landed and I began putting things in place for the exchange. I'd already paid cash for around 150,000 pills. Now I could make some calls and gather up the rest of what was needed.

D-Day was Wednesday 19th March 2003. I remember it very well—a sunny Spring day. I drove my Porsche to see my tattooist Jon in Guildford and ate some humble pie. I'd missed an appointment and I went to apologise. Jon was as easygoing as ever, cheerily booking me into his diary for a few hours of work the following week. As I left his studio, I said to him these exact words: "The only way I will miss that appointment, Jon, is if I'm dead or in prison!'

I'd chosen Danny, my best friend who had recently been working for me as a courier doing collections and deliveries of drugs and money, to help with the job because my other driver, Mark, had failed to get his lazy arse out of bed that morning. This was a regular thing with Mark, who was a good driver but a lousy timekeeper. Danny arrived at my house in the late morning and we went straight to work packing my BMW 'work' car with the vacuum-sealed bags of pills I'd bought for Steve. Once that was done, we killed time by having a bite to eat and then a workout. Eventually, it was time to make our way to the agreed meeting place where we would wait for Steve, Kevin and their entourage. Keeping the driving sensible and our eyes open for vehicles of the unwanted variety, namely those topped with blue lights, we left my place, met up with Ben and headed across Surrey—Danny in the BMW I'd bought him when he decided to work for me, Ben and me in one of my cars.

As a precaution, we took a back-lane route to our destination. The 40-minute trip went without a problem and, as we pulled into the industrial estate in West Byfleet, I glanced at my watch: we were early, as I always liked to be. Ben and I grabbed some food from one of the stores while at the same time, I looked out for the slightest sign of unwanted attention.

I'd asked Danny to hang back out of view, and he'd parked in a corner at the far end of the large and almost full parking area. Steve and his crew eventually pulled in. I greeted them with a quick handshake before we all set off in convoy towards their lock-up.

Steve wanted to do the exchange inside their warehouse a couple of miles away and I was fine with that. I'd already checked it out and was happy that it was sufficiently distant from prying eyes. I watched as one of his men unlocked and lifted the shutters, allowing their van to pull inside. The others moved to follow, but, as I went inside, I held up a hand signalling for them to wait outside by their vehicles instead.

Opening the rear doors of the van, I saw half a dozen large sports bags inside. Keeping a careful eye on my new business partners, I climbed in and pulled out a few bricks from each bag. They certainly looked the part—smooth, plastic-covered brown slabs weighing around nine ounces each, about seven inches long and an inch or so thick. It was definitely soap bar, so now it was just a question of the quality. I used the end of one bar to crack another in half cleanly down the middle as I'd done countless times before. Experience and the naked flame of my lighter held to the resin told me all I needed to know. The quality was slightly above average, not great, but selling it would be no problem.

I hardly noticed the first shouts, they seemed distant and were muffled... indecipherable. I definitely noticed them the second time, though; much louder, clearer and coming from people who were suddenly much closer.

'Armed police! Nobody fucking move!'

Instantly and without thinking, I jumped out of the van and sprinted towards the back of the poorly lit warehouse while Ben did the same. More noise now—loud shouting and fast, heavy footsteps that bounced around the walls of the dark warehouse, accompanied by flashes of red laser beams from semi-automatic weapons. I rounded a corner in the near dark and ran into Ben, almost sending us both to the floor. This was bad. I scrambled about some more, frantically scanning for an exit route before realising with a sinking heart that we were trapped. The warehouse, we now realised, had only one way in and one way out. I stopped moving and pressed my back flat against a wall, for now out of sight of anybody as the chaos continued with Ben. With me temporarily out of Old Bill's crosshairs, they focused solely on him

'Fuckin' put your fuckin' hands in the air! Keep still and get your fucking hands up!'

From the darkened recess where I now stood motionless, I watched and listened. A group of black-clad figures in full combat gear were edging towards Ben, semi-automatic weapons aimed at his chest. They screamed at him to 'get on the fucking floor! Lie face down, keep your fucking hands where we can see them!' Then, when he dropped to his knees they realised their view of him was blocked by a parked car. 'Fuckin' stand up! Stand up! Keep your fuckin' hands up!' It was a ridiculous moment as Ben pushed himself upright. In normal circumstances, it would have made me laugh but these circumstances were far from normal—we were up to our necks in shit. This was no time for comedy: these guys meant business. I stayed still and, as they crept towards Ben, the inevitable happened.

'One here!'

The copper had been shocked to see me out of the corner of his eye; it was as if they were so focused on Ben they'd actually forgotten about me. He'd spun quickly to his right and now the barrel of his gun was almost resting on the bridge of my nose. To this day I think about how easily he could have shot me dead—in that split second of catching sight of me he'd been spooked. It was as if somebody had crept up behind him and shouted, 'BOO!' into his ear. Instinctively, my hands went skywards in surrender, and within seconds three or four coppers had jumped on me, roughly shoving me to my knees and then laying me on my front. One heavy bastard rammed his knee into my back and used his weight to pin me in place while another grabbed my arms and twisted them up my spine.

As the bite of steel handcuffs locked firmly around my wrists, something happened that I've never forgotten—I was suddenly overwhelmed by a powerful feeling of peace and tranquillity that was almost hypnotic. I knew in that moment, as I lay helpless and trussed up on the cold, hard floor, that I'd lost all control of my life in an instant. There was nothing I could do as a free man any more, no choices available to me, no decisions to be made. It felt as if my life was over, and in a sense it was. On the one hand, it was a terrible, almost heartbreaking realisation, but, on the other, it was also strangely very calming. I'm not sure I've ever felt so relaxed before or since.

CHAPTER 2: POSH BOY, COMMON BOY

I was born in West London in August 1972. My early life was a patchwork of contrasts—I started out as an unwanted baby, but at nine months old I was transplanted into a land of relative luxury. It wasn't until I was nearly 30 that I uncovered the truth about my biological parents. An expensive but absolutely necessary journey of self-discovery in my late 20s revealed that my birth father was a Māori from New Zealand and my mother was an English girl from West London. For the formative years of my life, those details remained a mystery, and the only parents I knew were Bill and Sandra Ravenhill, the couple who welcomed me into their home before I was even a toddler. My new dad was a successful car dealer, my mum a horse-riding lady of leisure and housewife. They were both working-class Londoners who had made good, and we lived in the heart of Wentworth Golf Course—a private estate where these days the average house will cost you £15-20 million. In 2015, my sister told me she'd noticed our old house had just been sold. It was a relatively modest six-bedroom place with about three acres of garden and apple orchard—nothing spectacular when compared to some of the properties around us. It was, however, in the centre of the most coveted section of the estate, and the buyer in 2015 paid £15.5 million for it.

First and foremost, I was lucky to have made it out of the adoption lottery. My new mum, having just had a sudden and unexpected stay in hospital to have a kidney removed, discharged herself on the day I was 'delivered' and had to act like she was as fit as a fiddle. If the authorities had known the truth, the adoption would have been off for good—that kind of deception would have terminated the process. In pain, still bleeding but smiling through it all, Mum, with the help of my dad, managed to stay the course and I became Piers Ravenhill—named after Dad's friend Piers Courage, a Formula 1 driver who had been killed in a horrific crash during the Belgian Grand Prix in 1971. So now I had a name, a mum, a dad and a sister—Vanessa—who had been adopted not long before me. Born in 1970, my new sibling had been the victim of some terrible physical and emotional abuse by her natural parents before the powers that be stepped in and rescued her.

Growing up, I was blissfully unaware of the circumstances surrounding my adoption. Life as a young Ravenhill was, to an outsider looking in, very comfortable. My father's success in the car trade meant we lived well most of the time, although Dad's turbulent boom-and-bust business life occasionally caught up with him. One particular event, when I was about six years old, possibly shaped my early attitude towards people in authority. I was at home with my mum when a team of bailiffs turned up accompanied by a couple of police officers. Mum was screaming at them, then crying as she spoke to Dad on the phone while these intruders started removing furniture and other goods and placing them on our driveway. It's nearly half a century ago but I remember it like it was yesterday, watching in tearful silence and confusion as one of the coppers picked up my piggy bank and emptied the contents into his hand. He probably took about 25 pence in change—from a child!

I started at Virginia Water Junior School when I was four years old. I was very small, very shy but also, even at that stage of my life, feisty and prone to angry outbursts, although these were usually at home. I had a habit of breaking things in my rages—windows were a favourite. I was intelligent, though, apparently well above the average pupil, and my early school reports commented on this. The general message was, 'Piers is capable of anything in the classroom and could do great things if he actually sat still and concentrated once in a while.' This was the common theme for all of my school years. I could have been a grade-A student, and there were times when I put in the effort for a few weeks and showed it to everybody. On the whole, though, I didn't care about academia.

Early in my life, I developed a sense of not quite belonging or fitting in. I was happier in my own company and used to spend hours roaming the golf course alone and getting up to all sorts. At junior school, I also started to indulge in some rather dodgy behaviour. I started selling my toys—mostly Matchbox cars—to my classmates; a basic version of the wheeling and dealing that would become my trademark later on. These juvenile hijinks didn't go unnoticed by the schoolteachers. Mr Williams, the headmaster, even started calling me 'Pliers' because of my sticky fingers. Mum and Dad weren't exactly chuffed when they were called in to discuss my budding business ventures, but, bless them, they never came down too hard on me. I remember them being quite tickled by the whole thing—a reaction that, looking back, might have sent the wrong message. Dad was a wheeler-dealer, though—straight out of the Arthur Daley mould. Maybe he saw a bit of himself in what I'd been doing.

In retrospect, I can see that a lot of my behaviour as a kid was likely down to some deep-seated worries and insecurities. I was a chronic bed-wetter until I was about 12, which was both embarrassing and upsetting. Waking up in soggy sheets several times a week really did a number on my self-esteem.

My relationship with my parents, especially my dad, was a bit of a rollercoaster. He could be loving in his own way, but he had no patience for my constant antics and we butted heads a lot. I dreaded hearing him bellow my name when he came home from work, knowing a smack on the bum was probably coming. I accept that I deserved what I got a lot of the time, but I often felt as though my only interactions with him were for negative reasons. Mum was a bit softer, more of a hugger, but I saw from a very young age she had a temper that could match mine! In the middle of all the family drama, my sister Vanessa seemed to have an easier time of it. She was the archetypal daddy's girl and had a special bond with our father that I never had and never particularly wanted.

There was always a part of me that held back, that questioned who I was and where I really belonged. My doubts, confusion and irritability gained serious traction one day when I was about six. Mum and I were in the car, just the two of us, driving to Egham to do some shopping after she'd picked me up from school. Out of nowhere, she casually dropped a bombshell that would change everything. It was a moment I've never forgotten, almost like the, 'Where were you when you heard JFK had been shot?' question. 'I'm not your real mother,' she said, in the most matter-of-fact way. 'Your real mum didn't want you, so your dad and I took you in.' Her words were like a kick in the balls. Now, sitting alone in the backseat of this woman's, this *imposter*'s car, the feelings of not fitting in, my volatility, my at times deliberately provocative attitude... I think they were set in stone that day.

I wasn't just a misfit; I was an unwanted kid, dumped on this family because nobody else wanted me. The news shook me and, although I carried on with my life without giving it much thought until probably into my late 20s, I did reach an unhealthy conclusion about my parents in my teens. I decided after lots of pondering that my parents had 'bought' me the way you'd buy a pint of milk. I was a 'thing,' a possession and, just like they would use my dad's fortune to buy property abroad, my mum a new handbag or my dad his latest new Bentley or Rolls Royce, they had bought their children to complete their collection of luxury goods. Mum couldn't have children after cervical cancer in her teens had resulted in a hysterectomy, so in my mind, they used their wealth and status to get what they wanted.

These days I'm ashamed of myself for thinking that way about two people who, while I was never especially close to either of them, I have the utmost love and respect for. Knowing what I know now about the perils of the care system, I feel nothing but gratitude to them for probably saving me from the clutches of abusers and paedophiles that even today lurk en masse in the shadows of a system that is supposed to protect its vulnerable little humans.

All my life I've had a bee in my bonnet about the day my mum told me I wasn't hers. Hearing that my birth mother basically rejected me was a heavy blow for a six-year-old and the way she phrased it made it sound as if they took me in out of pity rather than love. I don't think she intended to be harsh but the scars from that conversation lasted long after the car ride ended.

As I tried to make sense of Mum's bombshell, other cracks started to show in our seemingly perfect life. When I was about 10, Dad's car business hit a rough patch, and he went bankrupt. Losing the business was a huge blow to our finances, and we had to say goodbye to the fancy life of Wentworth Golf Course. We lived for a few months in a friend's empty house in Ascot before finally moving to a converted farmhouse in Chertsey. It was a nice enough place, but it was a far cry from the upmarket side of Surrey that I was used to, and I felt the sting of our changed circumstances, mostly in the classroom.

By now I was at the exclusive Scaitcliffe Prep School in Englefield Green, located on Crown Estates property just outside Windsor Great Park. Scaitcliffe was a small school with about 120 pupils, most of whom were being readied for Eton, Harrow, St Paul's and all the other top public schools. I was there because my parents had decided after my dad's bankruptcy they could no longer afford to keep both me *and* my sister in private education. Again, they were maybe a little too liberal with the details of their decision-making, telling Vanessa and me that their choice to pay for my schooling was based purely on the fact that I was more intelligent than my sister and therefore a better long-term investment! This was in fact true. I was gifted academically, but Vanessa wasn't. She suffered from dyslexia, and in those days that made you a prime target for bullies—both pupils and teachers alike.

Really, though, they must have known they were taking a big gamble on me. I was bright and intelligent with an IQ of 149, but aged 10 I was still displaying a staggering lack of interest in the classroom. I could do it, I was very capable, and I put genuine effort into some subjects—French, Latin and ancient Greek in particular. But, even with those classes, I only performed strictly on my terms and, if I didn't fancy it, it simply wouldn't happen.

Money troubles aside, Dad's occasional run-ins with the law also cast a shadow over the family. I remember Mum telling me, again in her typically matter-of-fact style, that he'd been carted off to Pentonville prison for non-payment of fines—a result, I later learned, of him selling the same car to more than one person. Mum was left to pick up the pieces, selling some of Dad's cars for peanuts to get the money needed to get him out of jail. The whole episode was a harsh reminder of just how fragile our grip on the good life was at times. It was also a real lesson for me, one topic that even at the age of 10 I needed no more education in: people and how ruthless they can be when somebody else is in trouble. The buyers of my dad's stock—all long-term family friends—wasted no time in taking full advantage of a wife they knew was desperate. They smelled blood and swiftly moved in for the kill. To this day, when it comes to possessions and money, I trust nobody.

Dad's stint in prison was a turning point for our family, maybe the first time I saw cracks in the foundations. This event, coupled with Dad suffering the first of a series of heart attacks, signalled that things were changing for the Ravenhills, and things were certainly changing for me. I became progressively more insular and more withdrawn, channelling my anger into fights, petty theft and general rebelliousness. School, which in spite of my laissez-faire attitude to classwork was once a place I enjoyed (mostly because I was the star captain of the football and cricket teams, was vice-captain of the rugby team, was in the swimming team, the tennis team, the squash team and the athletics team!), started to feel like even more of a drag. I used to love boarding—being away from home was a relief for me. Now, though, my marks began to slip. I was flailing, and no one seemed to know how to get through to me.

It all came to a head, in a rather prophetic way, when I was 12. Mr Vickers, a semi-retired co-headmaster at my prep school, took Mum aside one day for a serious chat about my future. 'Mrs Ravenhill,' he said solemnly, 'this has only been said to one other pupil who attended this school before, and that was Richard Branson. Mark my words, your son will either be a millionaire or in prison by the time he's 30.' His words, eerily accurate in hindsight, were a sign of the rocky road ahead of me. The truth is I always took Mum's account of that conversation with a pinch of salt, thinking she probably invented it to try to get a bit more control over me and my behaviour. Years later, though, when I was 29 and lying next to a swimming pool in Gran Canaria with my then-girlfriend Janine, I was stunned to see it written in black and white. I was reading a biography by the celebrated journalist and author Tom Bower and it happened to be about Sir Richard Branson. In its pages—the pages that apparently Branson had tried to block publication of—was the story. When he left the well-heeled Stowe public school, it was said to him by his headmaster that he would be either a millionaire or in prison by the age of 30! Reading it gave me goosebumps, especially since at that time I was in fact a millionaire a couple of times over and I wasn't in prison... yet.

As I stood on the precipice of my teenage years, it was clear I was a kid adrift. The truth about my adoption, the money woes, Dad's jail time and my lack of social positioning (at home the kids called me 'posh boy,' at school the boys sometimes called me 'common boy,' 'orphan' or 'reject') had all taken a toll, chipping away at my already shaky sense of self. I was angry, insecure and increasingly drawn to the fun of misbehaving. Little did I know, these early dalliances with delinquency were just a preview of the criminal path I would soon be walking.

I was, in fact, already quietly tiptoeing along that criminal track when my family's world imploded. Driving home after a night out with my friend Nick and his girlfriend, we saw flashing blue lights and a crowd of people piled into the car park at Ravens, my Dad's nightclub on the A3 at Hindhead, Surrey. I knew something was amiss—this wasn't the typical low-level fuss of another scrap between the local Travellers and the squaddies who would travel to the club from Aldershot and other nearby garrisons. I had to stop and find out what was happening. Normally I would have been there anyway, working either behind the bar or, as I occasionally did, moonlighting as a doorman. This particular night though, 30th November 1991, I was free to go out and enjoy myself. As I left my car and told Nick I'd collect it from him the next day, I urged him to drive sensibly and winked as I told him he definitely did not want to be pulled over by the police, 'Not with what I've got hidden in here mate!'

Walking towards the melee, I gauged the noise and general restlessness of all the people as one or two began to recognise me. I heard my name called once or twice before suddenly a copper grabbed my arm. 'What are you doing?' I said as I spun around. 'This is my parents' place.'

'Are you Piers Ravenhill?'

'Yeah. Who are you?'

'Piers, can you just come with me for a moment, we want to talk to you. You're not in any trouble, we just need to have a quick chat.'

Now I saw people I knew well, doormen and bar staff from the club, looking at me, glancing towards one of the two ambulances parked outside the club entrance, then back to me. Jill, who'd worked for my parents for years, was crying. Something was wrong, very wrong. I broke free from the Old Bill and dashed straight to the first ambulance. To this day I wish I hadn't thrown its doors open; to this day I wish I could un-see what was going on inside. My dad was there, but I knew in an instant that he really wasn't there. His favourite white jumper was covered in blood that had come from his windpipe where paramedics had performed a tracheotomy in their frantic efforts to save him. I looked at his face, then glanced at the medical team's faces... and I knew.

Over the next few weeks, I watched nearly everybody who had been employed by my parents rob us blind. The nightclub was stripped bare by the live-in staff. The garage where my dad had been restoring and selling classic cars like Jaguar E-types, Daimler Darts and Triumph Spitfires was emptied by the blokes who my dad not only gave a living to but who had been friends with him since they were in their teens. I took my mum there one afternoon expecting to find the place locked and secure but ended up chasing one of the thieves with a hammer. At that moment I didn't give a shit what I did, and I was learning yet more lessons about my fellow human beings who I already had little time for; it was only Mum shouting at me that made me think twice. I stopped, put the hammer down, put my mum in the car and left the vultures picking at the bones of my family's wealth.

Amid all this chaos, we buried my dad, and I felt very little. I'm ashamed to say that not only did I plant my head firmly in the sand while the Ravenhill empire crumbled, but I also immersed myself in the drug dealing I had already been involved in for the past couple of years unbeknown to my dad, mum and sister. I had, in fact, told my mum on the night Dad died that I was a drug dealer—I don't know why exactly but I did.

By Christmas 1991, our fate was sealed and the truth about our business affairs had been brutally exposed. We were losing everything and it was all Dad's fault. He hadn't told anybody, not even my mum—his wife of 28 years—but not long before his death he had pulled yet another financial stroke. If he had just been relying on the nightclub takings to produce the £10,000 per month mortgage payments on the car garage, that would have been one thing. What he'd actually done though was use both the nightclub (which was bought and paid for) and our £500,000 family home (also bought and paid for) as security against the huge loan that paid for the garage. In 1991, there was a big recession on the horizon, my dad saw it coming, and he started to panic. We only saw this in hindsight but, once he died, unsurprisingly from a huge heart attack, the penny dropped.

From relative financial comfort and stability, we lost the lot pretty much overnight. When the Middle Eastern bank he'd borrowed from heard he had died, their response was swift and decisive. The loan was immediately called in, meaning nothing belonged to us any more. The club, the classic car garage and, worst of all, the house—all gone in the blink of an eye. I carried on running around like a headless chicken. My days at this time were all about selling drugs, taking drugs, getting drunk, getting into fights and taking no care of my mum or my sister.

Mum took a machete to all four corners of our house the day before we had to leave; she was like a woman possessed. I willingly obliged when she asked me to tell my New Age Traveller friends that the house would make a great squat for them and, by the time I visited them a few weeks into 1992, there were about 30 men, women and children plus a collection of dogs, cats and even pigs and ponies at the property. The place was being trashed by parties and hard living. I think it made my mum happy.

Whatever satisfaction Mum gained from knowing 'her' house was being ruined according to her wishes, it couldn't stop the freefall of her mental health. Two or three months after Dad's death she attempted suicide. She was found unconscious by my sister after swallowing a vast amount of pills, and she was saved by hospital staff before being sectioned to Farnham Road Hospital in Guildford. My response to this latest horror? I took her blood-red Mercedes Benz convertible and used it to deal more drugs while I showed off in it. Disgracefully, I didn't even have the manners or emotional attachment to visit her during her recovery and treatment.

In three short months, I'd lost my dad, my home (I'd moved back in after splitting with my girlfriend a few months before his death), nearly lost my mum... and I'd certainly lost any thoughts of living a respectable and legitimate working life. As I grappled with a cocktail of grief, anger and hatred in the wake of Dad's death, I found myself pulled deeper into the world of drug crime. What began as petty theft and drug dealing quickly escalated into something much more serious —a full-blown criminal enterprise that would consume my 20s and pave the way for my eventual fall from a great height.

9MILLION:

The seeds of my criminal destiny had been sown long before this dark chapter of my life, partly in the tumultuous soil of my unconventional upbringing. The feelings of rejection, the financial instability, the loss of my father—all these factors had come together to create a perfect storm, propelling me towards a life of crime. But, in those early days, I was oblivious to the larger forces at play, focused only on the next hustle, the next score. I had no idea that my early forays into the criminal underworld were merely the opening act of a grand and in some ways tragic drama that would unfold over the next 20 years. The lure of big money and the thrill of the fast life would be a siren song, drawing me ever deeper into a maze of vice and violence. Even as I threw myself headlong into this dark world, a part of me longed for something more—a sense of belonging, a purpose, a place to call my own. I knew I had talents and abilities that could potentially take me to the top of pretty much any ladder I set foot on. It just so happens that I chose to jump on the criminal ladder. It would be many years before I would come to understand the true cost of my choices, the toll they would take on not just my body, my mind and my soul but those of the people who actually loved me. But, in those early days, I felt invincible, untouchable—a young man with nothing to lose and everything to gain. The world was now mine for the taking, and I was hell-bent on grabbing it.

And so, as I once again stood as alone in the world as I had been when I was born, I prepared to embark on a journey that would take me to the heights of criminal success and the depths of personal despair. It was a path fraught with danger, but also one that held the promise of redemption. All I needed now was emotional strength and unwavering focus. Deep down I knew I had both; I had all of what I needed. I was different from my peers, I was not the average Joe. And now I was ready to show it.

CHAPTER 3: EARLY HUSTLES AND DISCOVERING MY CRIMINAL SIDE

Some kids dream of being astronauts or rock stars. Me? I wanted to be the next big thing in business. I was only about 12 when I took a chequebook from my mum's bag and made one out to myself... for £1 million. I still had my old headmaster's talk to Mum in my head. I guess I was a born hustler and to this day I like to have several income streams. A quid here, a quid there—the various earners have always kept me interested and stopped me from being bored.

It all started with Matchbox cars. At the tender age of seven, while my classmates at Virginia Water Junior School were content to simply race their toy vehicles around the playground, I saw an opportunity. With a few strategic trades and some savvy salesmanship, I soon had my first little business up and running. The other kids couldn't get enough of my wares, and I quickly learned that there was serious money to be made if you had the right product and the right hustle.

My juvenile hijinks didn't go unnoticed by the school teachers. Mr Williams, the headmaster, even started calling me 'Pliers' because of my sticky fingers. When he eventually spoke to my mum about it, he was decent and said he was quite impressed—but I had to stop. Mum and Dad weren't exactly chuffed when they were called in to discuss my budding business ventures, but, bless them, they never came down too hard on me. Dad thought it was amusing that his boy was now also a car dealer of sorts. He was a wheeler-dealer himself, straight out of the Arthur Daley mould, and maybe he saw a bit of himself in what I'd been doing.

As I grew older, my entrepreneurial spirit intensified. By the time I hit my teenage years, I was already well on my way to becoming a seasoned hustler. At 12, I discovered the fun to be had with alcohol, nicking bottles of wine, spirits and beer from the stockpile at my parents' latest business—the famous Ship Hotel in Shepperton, Middlesex. Some of this loot I would drink with my mate Richard as we walked from the Ship to the Walton Hop, a popular under-18s disco back then. The rest I would sell to mates at school to make sure I always had a few quid in my pocket to take myself to Stamford Bridge for the home games of my beloved Chelsea. It was a bit of a thrill, sneaking around and getting buzzed on stolen booze, but the real fun for me was getting that money safely in my pocket. This was just the beginning of a long and winding road into the world of crime.

By the time I left college at 18 with four A-levels (I never even bothered to collect my certificates!) and, despite my extracurricular activities, I landed my first proper employment and became a civil servant. It was a respectable job as an administration officer in the Unemployment

Benefits Office in Guildford. It was a decent job but the money was terrible and, even as I was doling out advice to the jobless and dealing with their benefit claims, I was already rising in the crime game. I knew there was a better way to make a living that didn't involve being threatened most days by penniless glue-sniffers!

I'd started smoking weed with my friends at 17, and it didn't take long for me to realise that I could make a tidy profit by selling to my mates. Why pay for my own supply when I could get others to foot the bill? It was a no-brainer. I quickly set about establishing myself as the go-to guy for puff in my now hometown of Hindhead, much to the annoyance of my so-called competition.

Soon enough, I was using my civil service job as a cover while doubling my income by selling weed on the side. It was almost too easy. My parents owned a nightclub, I was the new kid on the block in my area and I made sure I always had stuff to sell. I even had a mobile phone, which in the late '80s was quite something for a teenager.

As my confidence grew, so did my ambitions. I quickly graduated from selling weed to pushing harder stuff like amphetamines, ecstasy, acid and cocaine. I was still just a kid really, but I was already making some serious dough. My customer base expanded rapidly, stretching from sleepy Surrey villages to the neighbouring counties of Hampshire and West Sussex.

One of the keys to my success was my ability to build trusted relationships with my suppliers. I always paid in cash up front, never owing anyone a penny. This earned me a reputation as a reliable buyer and it also got me better prices. In the drug game, cash is king, and I had plenty of it.

By the time I hit 18, Ecstasy was the new big thing, and I was supplying big crowds at all-night raves in clubs far and wide, with a team of runners working under me. The money was rolling in faster than I could count it. Compared to the measly pay I got working the door or behind the bar at my folks' nightclub, drug dealing was a cinch. By this time, the civil service was a distant memory but I still had to keep up appearances. I took a job selling caravans for a while, working for a man called Michael Jordan at his dealership in Hindhead. But, even then, I couldn't resist the temptation to make a little extra cash on the side. I started nicking inventory from the lot and selling it off with the help of the equipment shop manager and my good friend—the one who first introduced me to smoking hash—Robert. It was all going swimmingly until I got caught with my hand in the till once too often. Jordan called me into his office and gave me the boot without ceremony. 'Get out. You're sacked,' he said, barely looking up from his paperwork. I didn't care. I knew I was destined for bigger and better things than flogging glorified tin cans on wheels. I told him to shove his job up his arse and proceeded to throw my framed Salesman of the Month award straight at him.

I won that award for selling a ridiculous number of new caravans at the Earls Court Caravan Show, where I was so successful it caused a salesman from another company to threaten to have my legs broken if I dared to gazump him again. That night, I told a 'business associate' what had happened and the next day at the show I watched as two of his boys—both fierce-looking heavyweights—read the upset salesman his fortune. One of them had the bloke by the arm as he pointed to me standing about 50 metres away and whispered in his ear. That angry caravan salesman kept out of my way for the rest of the week.

I realised then that the big cats I bought my goods from liked me. Looking back, it's easy for me to see why. I never owed a penny, never made a promise I didn't keep and over time I made these bosses, the people I aspired to be one of, money. I made them a lot of money.

I suppose most people expected me to outgrow my nefarious ways at some point—to turn my back on crime and join the ranks of the upstanding employed. But the lure of easy money was impossible to resist. Why start earning an honest living when I already had a very comfortable thing going on the shady side? Of course, this attitude landed me in all sorts of hot water with my parents, who believed their darling boy had the brains and ambition to go far in the 'real' world

'You'll be a solicitor and that's that,' my dad used to say.

'Why do you want me to be a solicitor?'

'Because they earn a fucking fortune! Paul [my dad's brief for around 20 years] has had tens of thousands from me. He's probably worth more than I am, the tight bastard!'

Somehow my folks remained unaware of the extent of my criminal dealings throughout my teens. Even a few minor run-ins with the law—usually for drinking, fighting and other disorderly conduct—never tipped them off that their lad was an up-and-coming drug dealer. With their heads buried firmly in the Surrey sand, they continued dreaming of a thoroughly respectable future for their adopted son. They were blissfully unaware that, while they were filling their staff with drinks and tallying up the night's takings at the club every weekend, I was cutting my teeth in an altogether different hospitality trade. Every day I was moving increasingly large parcels of drugs around the south of England, and every weekend I'd head off to the most popular raves, runners in tow armed with thousands of pills tucked into my jacket. The dance floor was my second shop and business was booming. I'd be happily getting off my tits—'High on my own supply' as Michelle Pfeiffer warned against in the hit Al Pacino film *Scarface*—while at the same time, I was earning thousands a night from Es that punters happily paid £20 a pop for.

The early '90s rave scene in the southeast was like a gold rush for business-minded dealers like me. It was almost too easy. A few pills here, a few wraps there. Before you could say, 'Big fish, little fish, cardboard box,' I'd doubled or tripled my money. With the right tunes blasting and the party in full swing, 'heads' would practically throw their cash at you, barely pausing to check what they were getting.

With every weekend that passed, my ambitions grew, along with my clientele and my profits. Before long, I was set to become the go-to guy in an ever-expanding area. To some people, I was a kind of countercultural hero, someone to be admired, but I never listened to or gave a toss about any of that stuff. I don't have a big ego and I've never needed it massaged. I was all about the money, I never wanted to be a celebrity bad boy.

What I failed to consider, though—and I'm ashamed of this because I'm a thinker, a deep thinker, in fact—was that every high has its comedown. And mine was hurtling towards me at breakneck speed. A friend once said to me something that stuck in my head in the way that certain things do for all of us: 'If you're at it, if you're making money from drugs, your sentence is already in the post. The only question is, When will it land on your doormat?'

But, before the curtain came crashing down on my fledgling empire, I had a few more chapters to write in my book of youthful misadventures. As I plotted my next moves, I couldn't help but reflect on how far I'd come in such a short time. From flogging toy cars in the schoolyard to shifting serious lumps of coke, MDMA, Ecstasy pills, weed, hash, I sold anything and everything. Well, almost. I always drew the line at crack and heroin, and I never got involved with them. Believe it or not, I do have morals, and I accept now that my thinking was a bit off-kilter, but I refused to buy and sell them because, as far as I was concerned, they were the only drugs that caused problems for both their users and the wider public.

So far, being in the drugs game had been one hell of a ride, but deep down I knew this was in some ways only the beginning. The real test was yet to come. Could I make it as a major player in the cutthroat world of wholesale drug trafficking? Did I have the guts, the guile and the sheer bloodymindedness to join the big boys at their dinner table?

These were the questions that I asked myself while in reality, it was already happening; reputation and business sense were powerful catalysts in the underworld and I was fortunate to have plenty of both. The last major ingredient was buying power, and again my natural inclination to reinvest the vast majority of my profits would now bear more fruit.

For now, let's just say that my transformation from mid-level dealer to fully-fledged drug lord was about to begin in earnest. And, if I thought I knew everything there was to know about the game... well, hindsight is a wonderful thing, as clear as crystal.

CHAPTER 4: EXPANDING MY CRIMINAL ENTERPRISES

I've always been told, and in spite of my relatively low self-esteem, I've always known deep down, that I could have—still can—make a success of pretty much anything I turn my hand to. It just happened to be that I chose crime. I'm not really sure how it even happened, and in some ways, I think the game chose me. I certainly didn't wake up one morning and suddenly have the notion, 'This is how I'm going to make my fortune.' It was more of a steady growth and evolution. The thing that set me apart and gave me the edge over other dealers was that I never took time off. My work phones never left my side and were never switched off. It used to drive my girlfriend nuts, but it was my *MO* and anyone who didn't like it just had to take a deep breath and lump it. You see, I had something of a talent for the whole drug-dealing lark. It came naturally to me, like breathing. I'd started small, of course, flogging a bit of weed to my mates and reinvesting the profits, but, as the rave scene exploded in the late '80s and early '90s, I saw an opportunity to expand my operation and nurture a new income stream to run alongside what I already had. I ventured into new markets, supplying party pills and other illicit favours to the dealers supplying the hordes of wide-eyed, sweaty-palmed ravers who couldn't get enough of the stuff.

As my reputation grew, so did my network of contacts. I was introduced to bigger players in the game, suppliers who could provide me with the quantity and quality of products I needed to keep up with demand. I had storage units scattered across the southeast, stuffed full of every drug imaginable. Well, almost every drug; as I've already mentioned, crack cocaine and heroin were strictly off my menu. Everything else, though, was fair game.

I was a hands-on boss. I never paid or asked anybody to do something I wouldn't do myself. I always believed that a top dog should lead by example and that's exactly what I did. There were also plenty of things, most of the bigger and top-end deals, that only I was privy to. I paid my people on time and I paid them well, but some of my business was definitely strictly on a need-to-know basis, and some of it they didn't need to know. Why? Because even though they were in the loop for all the day-to-day business and through that alone they got a pretty clear picture of how much I was making. I've never trusted people, even those I simply had to trust, so the big stuff—deals that were netting me £50,000 or £100,000—I did undercover. Probably partly due to my trust issues, I also wanted to be involved in every aspect of the nine-to-five operation, from sourcing the product to overseeing distribution. I paid my team well for their discretion and loyalty.

Even with my fingers in every pie, though, I couldn't be everywhere at once. That's where my little café came in handy. It was the perfect front for my less-than-legal activities, a place where I could discreetly chat with suppliers and clients while I cooked them a meal or made them a cappuccino. To the casual observer, I was just another small-business owner trying to make an honest living.

Despite my growing success, I was determined to remain independent. I didn't want to be beholden to any bosses or crime families. I was my own man, and I intended to keep it that way. I cultivated an image of professionalism and reliability among my suppliers and my clientele, and I consistently turned down some of the real 'faces' in the game. The people I worked with, I did so because I specifically chose to work with them—it was never the other way around. Nobody was in a position to 'choose' me, though one or two tried over the years. The firms above me on the ladder knew they could count on me to be ultra-discreet, turn up on time or early and always pay cash on delivery, whether it was £10,000 or half a million. The people below me, my punters, knew they could rely on me to deliver on time, not take the piss with prices or quality, and sometimes help them out if their operation hit a snag.

As the money poured in, I started living well. I didn't ram it down people's throats, but I did buy top-end cars, motorbikes, jewellery and watches plus a lot of the latest gadgets. Shouting my mouth off, becoming wrapped up in my own hype or flaunting the wealth too ostentatiously—I left that to others and often watched as they got themselves nicked and lost the lot. I kept a low profile, never drawing too much attention to myself or my activities. Whenever Mark, one of my most trusted drivers, remarked on the sheer volume of cash flowing through my hands, I played it down. 'Just another day at the office, mate. If only all this money was mine, but sadly it isn't,' I quipped, trying to sound nonchalant.

My operation had grown far beyond the small-time deals of my youth. By 2003, aged 30 and at the height of my criminal career, I was stashing away around £1 million in profits annually. In 2002, taking into account the inevitable losses that all businesses suffer, I still bought a new Porsche 911, a new BMW, several new motorbikes and all kinds of other treats. That year, I was sitting on a beach in Dubai while staying at the Burj Al Arab Hotel when my work phone rang. A quick and almost monosyllabic chat, and then I switched it off and put it away. My girlfriend Janine knew something was amiss.

'What's wrong?' she said. 'You never switch that bloody thing off.'

'Nothing—drink your cocktail.'

'Don't give me that. What's happened?'

'Let's just say the cost of this holiday has just shot up from about fifteen grand to about a hundred!'

The call was to tell me an £85,000 consignment of hash had been intercepted by customs at one of our ports. Despite that loss and one or two others in 2002, and despite the spending, I still tucked away £978,000 of clear profit. I'd say I was at the top, whatever that really means. But with great wealth comes great responsibility, even greater risks and a wider range of pressures.

I knew I was playing a dangerous game. The law was always nipping at my heels, waiting for me to make a mistake. And there was always the threat of betrayal or treachery. I watched everyone around me carefully day in, day out, looking for even the tiniest sign that someone was plotting to sell me down the river and take my crown.

The key for me was always secrecy. As I mentioned earlier, I kept my crew on a need-to-know basis. Not even my inner circle, the people deeply immersed in the part of my life that wasn't crime, none of them were privy to the full scope of my operations; not my mum, not Janine (she didn't even know I was a drug dealer!), nobody. Danny and Mark, my two most reliable couriers, knew better than to ask too many questions about the origins or destinations of their cargo. They just did their jobs efficiently and discreetly, which kept the wheels turning smoothly.

I also had a strict policy of not mixing business with pleasure—and there were no exceptions. Janine thought I was a legitimate businessman. She was an intelligent woman and may have had some private ideas about me as a businessman-cum-personal trainer, but she was kept in the dark about everything. It's not that I didn't trust her; I just didn't want to burden her with the weight of my choices.

As I reflect on this part of my life, I can't help but shake my head at the recklessness of my younger self. The chances I took, the boundaries I pushed—it all seems so over the top now with the benefit of hindsight. At the time, though, I was doing what I chose to do, I was doing it well and certainly not spending much time thinking about the possible negative outcomes if things started to go wrong. Things didn't go wrong for me. Obviously, all businesses have peaks and troughs, and it was never completely plain sailing day in, day out, but, generally speaking, I spent the whole of my 20s running my criminal enterprises in the same way that I ran my straight business and I was on a consistently upwards trajectory.

That's the folly of youth though. I never really had a plan B because, the way I saw it, I didn't need one. My thoughts were seldom focused on what to do if something bad happened; they were only concentrated on expanding the business, selling more drugs in larger amounts and making more money. I'm not saying I never thought about the possibility of ending up in trouble with the law. I had to at times—for example, immediately after the two or three times I was pulled over by the police who, mostly just by luck, *didn't* find what was sitting in the car with me. On one occasion, I was stopped by police in West London as I headed back to Surrey following a 'business' meeting. I wasn't even meant to be at the meeting, which was in reality a simple collection of quite a large amount of soap bar Moroccan hash, but a driver had let me down at short notice and forced me to get my hands dirty. The police took my details and checked them on the Police National Computer database, then had a brief root through the front and back of the car. I kept cool as they asked their questions, and it wasn't long before they sent me on my way. As I calmly headed towards the M3 motorway that would take me home, I wondered why they hadn't looked inside the boot. If they had, it would have been game over, but they missed the 250 kg I'd just picked up and paid for.

My criminal enterprises had reached their summit by the early 2000s. I was riding high on my success and had various interests and involvements, but little did I know that I was about to come crashing to earth with a huge bump. The authorities would soon have me firmly in their sights once they'd decided it was time to take me down. I certainly had some dark and difficult days coming my way thanks to the NCS and the police forces of Surrey, Hampshire and West Sussex. I didn't know it when I exploited the non-status mortgage loophole to buy my new house in Ash, Surrey, with a huge deposit that kept the employment status questions to a minimum, but my activities were already being quietly monitored. It wasn't long before I would find out that crime *doesn't* pay, at least not in the long run. I was making a killing during my heyday as a drug kingpin, but at what cost? My freedom? My relationships with loved ones? The fortune I had amassed? Or all of those things?

Don't get me wrong: I never thought I was invincible, untouchable. I just didn't really give it much thought as I marched on. I was as careful as the next man. I took my liberty and the liberty of those working for me very seriously at all times, but the reality is that when they come for you, they methodically expose all the little chinks in your armour before moving in for the kill.

Most crucially, there is always a choice. I chose this path for myself; no one twisted my arm. But looking back now with the wisdom of age and experience, I realise that there were other roads I could have taken, other futures I could have embraced

9MILLION:

had I had enough self-awareness to see them at the time. But hindsight is a wonderful thing, as they say.

CHAPTER 5: PLAYING WITH FIRE

They say a rising tide lifts all boats, and in my case, the surging waves of cash were certainly keeping my yacht afloat. Business was thriving, and my empire was expanding fast. I was riding high, but what I failed to sense was that I was about to be swallowed up by a tsunami. As the old adage goes: 'More money, more problems.' The larger my operation became, the more I had to keep glancing over my shoulder. It wasn't just the police I was concerned about; there were plenty of other predators in the sea ready to sink their teeth into my profits. I knew I had to safeguard what I'd built, and that meant arming myself.

In 2002, I was hearing whispers in the area, which at the time was pretty much the heartland of the British Army, that a small team of ex-squaddies was making its own mark in a novel way. The grapevine was telling me this team was using the training Her Majesty the Queen had blessed them with to shadow and then rob higher-end drug dealers. They were armed, organised and efficient, and had taken some big scores of drugs, cash, watches and jewellery. They were also, I was told by a reliable source, quick to use violence and had no qualms about threatening and even hurting wives and girlfriends. Their methods were simple but effective: a few weeks of reconnaissance before going in fast and hard on their target. They stuck to their meticulous plans and were gone in a flash.

To be honest, these ex-soldiers were not the only reason I started to build myself a little arsenal, but they played a part. Guns and drug dealers—even in leafy Surrey they can go together like peaches and cream, which they did for me. When I heard about the exploits of the ex-military band of brothers, I already had at my disposal a sawn-off shotgun, a collection of cans of CS gas and a 50,000-volt stun gun, all kept physically within easy reach. Within days of the first talk of other dealers being robbed, I'd added a Swiss/German SIG Sauer P228 9mm handgun and a small, recommissioned Bauer automatic that fitted snugly into the centre console of my work car. A friend and business associate came for dinner at my house one evening and asked, 'Why do you keep a loaded weapon in the drawer?' when he sat at the coffee table in my lounge. I told him that, if these robbing bastards were going to come through my door waving guns about in my house, they needed to be prepared to use them, because I was definitely going to use mine. Fortunately, I never had to test my resolve.

I did use my weapons, very occasionally, during my everyday life as a criminal, but I never fired a gun at anybody. I'm not proud of it but I can't lie about it, can't say I didn't cock one and hold it in one or two faces over the years, but those faces were owned by chancers who weren't paying their (substantial) drug bills in good time, or even worse they had got it into their poorly developed brains that I would let them get away with their bright idea of simply not paying it at all.

In those days, I wasn't a particularly violent man but I always had it in my head that the underworld was watching, and if I let one fool get away with it more idiots would be queueing up to repeat the trick. One time I had to deal with a bloke in Portsmouth who, before the crack pipe got hold of him, had been a big player on the south coast. He owed me about £30,000 for a kilo of coke, and one Saturday night I finally got fed up with his bullshit excuses and decided I would deal with him personally. I picked up the SIG Sauer, chucked Danny my car keys and headed for Pompey. Gun in hand, I knocked on the door of this grubby little council flat and the man I was looking for opened it. His face dropped like a knackered lift when without saying anything I lifted my arm so that I was now aiming at his nether regions. He beckoned me in and I watched him very carefully as he reached into a drawer and pulled out a bag.

'How much is it?' I asked as he handed it to me.

'Twenty grand.'

'Well, where the fuck is the rest? Please don't think for a second I'm here to be shortchanged. You'd better start making phone calls, my friend.' The call he made was, in fact, only a shout to another room, to his girlfriend: 'Bring that bag of white through to me!'

I left with the £20,000 and about half a kilo of coke, and Danny got us back to my house in time for *Match of the Day*. The coke had been re-pressed to within an inch of its life, but by the time it was sold that man's bill was settled and we never spoke again.

But it wasn't just the guns that were multiplying like rabbits. The money was stacking up so fast I was starting to run out of places to store it. I had around a quarter of a million pounds buried in containers all around my garden, plus hundreds of thousands placed with trusted friends and even some family members.

It was getting ridiculous, but I was now starting to think about my retirement from the game. At Christmas 2002, I sat in my study at home and worked out my earnings for the year. When I saw how well I'd done, it was the tipping point. I'd been mulling over the idea of going into property and the numbers on my piece of paper made my mind up—I was getting out of crime; I didn't need it any more. I had enough money to make some investments and more than enough to live comfortably while the seeds I planted germinated and then grew. Over the next few days, I did some more thinking, about Ben, Mark, Danny and one or two other 'employees.' I felt bad, not because they depended on me for their livelihoods—they were all working people in their own right—but because they were in theory about to watch me ride off into the sunset with my millions bursting my saddlebags.

By New Year's Eve, I'd slightly changed my plans. I could trim the drugs round down to only the best and most reliable customers and still earn comfortably £20,000 a week. My idea now was to hand over almost complete control to the three amigos, give the two who shall remain anonymous a golden goodbye of £100,000 each and almost 'retire.' Ben, Mark and Danny would now run the entire operation, earn £5,000 a week each and have access to *all* of my contacts, many of whom they had no idea even existed. The remaining £5,000 of weekly profit—that would go to me.

I'd built this business and it was very profitable, but of course, it was very rarely plain sailing. They were still going to need me as a point of reference for all the little details that they wouldn't be able to master overnight: logistics, cash flow, problem-solving. On top of that, they'd need me to show them the best ways to interact with all the various personalities on both the customer and supplier fronts. It was also inevitable that one or two associates, who I knew would be very reluctant to deal with anybody other than me, would be left for me to speak to until they felt comfortable with the new setup. I liked this plan: I could get on with my property ideas and they could get on with keeping the business moving forwards. I estimated it would be around a year before they didn't need me any more. To me, at Christmas 2002, this seemed like a sensible and well-thought-out plan.

By 1st January 2003, I'd chucked it all out of the window! One trusted confidante told me that, if I was seriously just going to turn my back on a net profit of £20,000 a week and give it all away, I was mad. A few days after that conversation, I changed my mind and dropped the idea. I sometimes ask myself whether I was just plain greedy, which I don't think I was, or just plain stupid, which I suppose I must have been. The truth is, no matter what I decided, all of us were already nicked; we just didn't know it yet. Operation Sculpture was in full flow, led by the NCS and backed up by the police forces I mentioned before: Surrey, Hampshire and West Sussex.

9MILLION:

My setup had all the gear: hydraulic presses for compacting the drugs, mixing agents to cut the product, counting machines to keep track of the pills, you name it. They even found testing kits, scales, gloves and a radio scanner, making it clear just how professional my operation was.

CHAPTER 6: NCS

Everything carried on as it always had. It was a frantic time, juggling the supply, the cash and the constant need to stay one step ahead of my rivals and the law. I had a storage unit where I kept the really big stashes, but even that wasn't enough sometimes. The money and the product just kept flooding in, and I was constantly on the lookout for new hiding spots. Apart from the containers of cash already buried around my garden, I was now paying trusted friends a few quid to keep cashboxes and suitcases stuffed with pound notes and euros in their houses—sometimes literally under their beds!

I was playing a dangerous game. The more I had, the more I wanted to protect it, and that meant taking bigger and bigger risks. But when you're in the thick of it, you don't stop to consider the consequences. You just keep chasing that next big score... until it all comes crashing down.

The day they came for me, I thought I was as ready as I could be. I had my guns, my loyal crew, my stashes hidden away. But I was up against a different kind of beast with a different objective this time.

The NCS had been watching us closely. During their undercover operation, they'd observed me involved with stolen high-value cars that had had their identities changed and new documents. They'd seen me going in and out of my locked storage unit, the one accessed with considerable difficulty, where they later found the vast majority of my drug stock.

When they finally made their move, they came in hard. All those raids (more than 500 police officers, some armed with guns and all of them armed with warrants, searched more than 40 addresses across the south of England in a coordinated sweep whereby the properties' doors were all taken off their hinges at exactly the same time once I was safely in handcuffs), all the seizures of drugs, money, valuables and firearms they then gathered hastily together and transported to the outside of Ben's gym for a photo shoot and plenty of back-slapping among their smug selves.

While all this was going on, my mum was also being given a very hard time for no reason. They knew very well who was involved and who wasn't, but nevertheless, NCS thought it a worthwhile use of taxpayers' money to kick in her door as well. This wasn't any old raid though; they used the same black-clad 'stormtroopers' who had earlier that day swept up me and Ben. Armed and abusive, they waved their weapons in my mum's small, one-bedroom flat, called her a 'cunt' and told her she was going to prison just like her 'little boy.' My mum didn't stand for it, afterwards telling me she thoroughly enjoyed herself as she turned the air blue while slinging various ornaments at the invaders of her home.

My sister, living with her husband and baby son in Gosport, Hampshire, was also given the treatment. It wasn't armed police for this one, but they smashed her front door off its hinges and proceeded to pull my sleeping brother-in-law

Graham out of bed, handcuff him and march him down the street in front of all their neighbours, wearing only his boxer shorts. Needless to say, he was later released without charge.

*

The day I was nicked in West Byfleet, I was kept in the warehouse for a long time after they'd taken Ben away. Put down on my knees and surrounded by armed coppers in balaclavas, I could feel my hands were swollen and my wrists in pain. They'd been overenthusiastic, but I kept my mouth shut. I listened as I heard voices in the distance, but mostly I was alone with my thoughts as my mind raced. Finally, I was taken outside, photographed, and then shoved into the back of a marked Volvo estate, with an armed stormtrooper on either side of me. As we set off in the middle of what was now a convoy of three police cars, I noticed the sounds of a helicopter above. I thought it was all a bit over the top, but there was more to come. With flashing blue lights and sirens blaring, we cut straight through all the early evening traffic and made it to Guildford police station in what felt like no time.

At the station, I was marched straight into an office where a man in a uniform decorated with all kinds of medals and ribbons sat waiting for me at his desk. He introduced himself as Assistant Chief Constable of Surrey Police, said I had to officially be told by the highest ranked officer available, which he was, that I was being held incommunicado until further notice: no telephone call, no solicitor. I looked at him with a blank face because this was all new to me. I could easily have asked him, 'Is that good or bad?' because I didn't have a clue what it meant. Maybe I should have thanked him for using his power to arrange that nobody bothered me while I quietly assessed the severity of the situation I was now in!

Next, I was walked to a police cell. The door was unlocked and I was ushered inside. A man in a cheap suit stood up and said, 'Hello, Piers, my name is Gary Parkin and I'll be dealing with the removal of all your assets and property.' I said nothing but I remember thinking, 'Hang on, mate, I haven't even been charged with anything yet.'

He seemed to read my mind. 'You're looking at 25 years, Piers,' he said. I kept my poker face firmly fixed and my hands by my side as he offered his to me. As he left, he said, 'I'll put it very simply for you, Piers—don't fuck with me and I won't fuck with you.'

As I sat on a cold wooden bench, my mind started racing. I knew I was in a lot of trouble and I battled the blitz of negative thoughts. That night was long and lonely, made especially long by the occupant of the cell next to mine. 'Screaming banshee' barely describes the woman who, in my opinion, they'd placed deliberately into the mix—a drug addict clearly suffering withdrawal symptoms. She never stopped shouting and banging on her cell door, demanding cigarettes and pleading to see a nurse. They could have put her in any number of other cells but they thought it best to park her as close to me as possible. I guess they thought it both amusing and a large dose of poetic justice: drug dealer finally gets justice direct from one his victims.

In the early evening of the following day, I was allowed to speak to a duty solicitor on the phone. I gave him a brief outline of events and asked him to come and see me. His name was Gerald Elvidge—he was officially a family lawyer, but I felt comfortable talking to him and asked him to represent me. When I was finally taken for my first interview under caution, he was by my side, and NCS played another of the cards they had up their sleeve.

I'd been told that every person detained by NCS under the Operation Sculpture banner had been taken to separate police stations across the south east, but there was one planned exception. As Gerald and I were led through the custody suite towards the interview rooms there, sitting huddled up and crying on a bench, was my girlfriend, Janine. I can't imagine what she was thinking as they marched me past her, especially as she'd been completely in the dark about my secret life of crime, but I was definitely thinking this had been done on purpose. 'Tell these cunts they will not get me into an interview room all the time she is in this building,' I whispered to Gerald.

An hour or so later, Gerald came to my cell door to tell me Janine had been bailed pending further investigation, and we were ready for Old Bill's questions. As advised, I said 'no comment' to almost everything. We went on for nearly nine hours and by the end I was amazed at how tiring sitting on a chair exerting no energy had been. What I got from it, though, was an idea of just how much trouble lay ahead. I knew it was plenty before the interviews, but they gave us so much detail about the extent of Operation Sculpture that it really hit home.

Another little kick in the balls came mid-interview when there was a knock on the door. The recording was paused as two suited coppers came in to tell Gerald, and therefore me, they'd be charging me for two more kilos of coke that had been dug up in my garden along with what they said was a substantial amount of cash. That substantial amount of cash was—I know because I'd put it there—£93,000 in £50 notes.

After the interview, I spent another night in the cell and this time they didn't play the clucking junkie card on me. The following morning I was formally charged with... I can't remember what, but Gerald said they were just holding charges until the Crown Prosecution Service (CPS) decided what the real charges would be. It had been nearly three days now and I was shattered; very little sleep, one cold shower and an introduction to the vile toothpaste and pointless toothbrushes I'd now be using in prison for the foreseeable future.

Chained to a giant of a security guard, I was led to my first experience of a 'sweatbox,' one of the rectangular white buses with blacked-out windows we all see on our roads. The drive from Guildford to Woking Magistrates' Court was about half an hour—plenty long enough for me to be sick on my cubicle floor.

CHAPTER 7: THE STENCH OF REALITY

Sitting in a cold and soulless holding cell at Woking Magistrates' Court gave me more time to think, and most of that time I spent frying my own brain with what-ifs and a heavy dose of 'would have, could have, should have.' After an hour or so, I heard the jangling of keys and the sound of voices—one of them I thought was familiar. I called out as the door next to mine slammed shut, 'Spud? Ben, is that you?'

'Fuckin' hell. Pete?' (I used a new name when I moved into my new area—always mindful of informants.) We exchanged details of our experiences, the conversation taking twists and turns until he asked me what the police had said to me. 'They've told me I'm getting 25 years, mate.'

I can't give you a plausible reason why, but when I said those words we both burst into hysterical laughter. I wonder if it was a form of tension release, but it was totally inappropriate. We were in so much trouble, and it definitely was not funny.

Slowly over the next hour or so more co-accused arrived. None of us were put in cells together, so very quickly the whole area became an acoustic nightmare of around eight or nine people shouting to be heard.

Finally, we were all ushered into the dock of one court. I looked along the line and saw faces I didn't even recognise, but mostly I looked at my mum and some other familiar faces in the public seating area. We were in and out of the court in under five minutes. Gerald had told me he wouldn't waste the court's time by applying for bail. I had zero chance of getting it. This size of operation, this amount of drugs... it was never going to be a case of a magistrate saying, 'Yeah, go home. We'll give you a shout when we need you back!'

Me, Ben and Danny were remanded into custody. As I left the dock, I looked at my people across the room and held up a photograph of my six-year-old daughter that Mum had brought to Guildford police station in a sports bag full of clothes and toiletries.

The journey to HMP High Down was gruelling. Nausea gripped me as we crawled around the M25. I was shaking, sweating and occasionally retching into a sick bag. The three of us randomly broke into singing *Always Look On the Bright Side of Life* at one point. The only words from the fourth guy on the journey were, 'Tell the fuckin' driver to get a move on, mate. I wanna be back in my cell for *EastEnders*!'

It took about two hours to cover the 25 miles to High Down. It was the only jail I'd ever set foot inside before, the difference that day being that once I'd helped my friend's girlfriend deliver the ounce of hash that he, in a packed visits hall, grabbed and shoved up his arse faster than a rat goes up a drainpipe, I could get up and leave. When I'd be leaving this time nobody could say. I thought about the police goading me with their '25 stretch' predictions. I knew nothing about prison and sentencing back then, so in my head, I would be 55 when I left this mess if they were right.

It took another couple of hours for us to be processed in reception. I was drained when I was finally given a plastic bag with some tatty old bedding inside. I held it in one hand while a plastic plate of cold food was shoved into the other. It was around 9 p.m. when the three of us were led onto the induction wing, officially called Houseblock 3.

Things became real as I scanned the wing. It was miserable looking and grey, a giant box of metal, artificial light and the air smelled of a hundred bedrooms the morning after the night before. Noise bounced around high walls from various sources. I was led to a cell door, which the screw opened. It was dark inside. He flicked the light on and from the far side of this small container, there was sudden movement in a small bed. A bloke who came out from under his blanket, shot me a menacing look then disappeared again without saying a word. I'd woken this fella up and I don't think he was very pleased about it. I walked in and the door slammed behind me. I tiptoed towards the second bed and sat down in the dark, even trying to chew my food quietly. I left most of it because it was... well, it was exactly what I should have expected—a physical taste of what was now my new life.

Eventually, I got up and headed for the toilet cubicle for a pee. I opened the small door and was hit by the most vile stench. I didn't know where it was from, but I'd never known anything remotely like it, and I've never forgotten it. At around 10 o'clock, I pulled out the prison blanket, lay down fully clothed and drifted away.

CHAPTER 8: YOU CAN RUN BUT...

I was woken by squawking at first light: the sound of the resident crows collecting all the food thrown out of cell windows. My cellmate stirred as the rest of the wing started to wake up and make noise. His first words to me were, 'Got any burn, bruv?' I pulled out the 'smokers pack' I'd been offered by the screws in reception and lobbed it onto his bed before going to the toilet. Opening the door was as gruesome as it had been the first time. I stood in the cubicle and a quick look revealed the problem—my new friend's trainers. Festering is probably a fair word to use. We chatted briefly and he told me his name was Matt. He'd just been nicked for an armed robbery on his local Tesco petrol station. Matt was a drug addict and he'd made a pointless move with only one possible outcome to get a few quid for a hit. He thought the cashier had recognised him even though he'd covered his face with his scarf.

At around nine o'clock the cell door was unlocked. A steady buildup of noise on the landings finally got the better of me and I poked my head outside. There was Ben, leaning on the iron railings outside his cell directly opposite mine. He saw me, rolled his eyes and let out a big breath. His cellmate—a Traveller who had kept him awake for half the night protesting his innocence—had been banging on again that morning about the 'unfair' three-year sentence he'd just been given for possession of a firearm. I don't suppose Ben wanted to hear that kind of stuff on his first night in jail—not with the sentences we were looking at.

We went outside for some fresh air when the screws called exercise and found Danny in the yard. I felt for him because he'd been placed on a different part of the wing, meaning we'd only see him either in that yard or occasionally at mealtimes. He was quiet—missing his family, girlfriend and his packets of cigarettes. I gave him some tobacco as we walked around the yard with Ben.

*

The most common piece of advice we were given during our brief stay in High Down was, 'Do whatever it takes. Don't let them take you to Belmarsh.' Our case was transferred to the Central Criminal Court, better known as the Old Bailey, within a couple of days of our arrest. This was most likely down to the size of Operation Sculpture, which caused ripples across the southeast and had been reported by some of the national newspapers. Me, Danny and Ben—now sharing a three-up cell after some polite asking of the right screws—all knew Belmarsh was inevitable sooner or later. The Old Bailey was served by Belmarsh, meaning this was the jail that defendants on trial there were produced from.

Soon after we landed in High Down we were given a date for an appearance at the Bailey, but before that time came, I had an unwelcome visit. Our cell door was opened one morning.

'Ravenhill, legal visit.'

'I don't think that's right, guv. I haven't heard anything from my solicitor.'

He scanned his paperwork.

'Piers Ravenhill JC7187—is that you?'

'Yes, guv.'

'You have a legal visit this morning.'

On my way to the visits hall, I wondered if Gerald maybe had some important news about our case. Or more bad news to add to the huge pile I'd already amassed. At the visits hall, I was shown into a small room where two men were waiting, neither of them Gerald.

'Hello, Piers. Take a seat.'

'Where's Gerald?'

'Piers, we're from National Crime Squad. We're not really here to talk about your case, we're here to help you.'

I gave these two coppers my best poker face.

'I think you've already done enough for me and my family, thanks. I don't want or need anything from you lot.'

'Well, you know you are looking at 25 years, don't you? The reason we're here is because we can give you all sorts of help through it all. If you give us some information, we'd look at getting you a reduced sentence and move you to a more comfortable prison. We can even help your family financially.'

I looked both these men in their eyes.

'You mean you want me to be a grass? Are you fucking serious?'

I stood up and moved towards the door before hitting the glass part with my palm to get the screws' attention and get the fuck out of this so-called 'legal visit.'

'So you don't want to talk to us, Piers?'

I turned round to see the senior of these two coppers reach for the inside pocket of his jacket. He pulled out a cheap-looking business card, placed it on the table and slid it towards me.

'When you change your mind, call me on this number.'

I moved my hand and placed my finger on the card, gently sliding it back.

'Never gonna happen, mate. I'm no fuckin' grass, and if I have to do 25 years, so be it. I'll get out of prison and every day between now and then I'll be able to look myself in the mirror and know that I kept my principles intact.'

I was never contacted by them again.

After around a week inside, the screws came to our cell door around 6 a.m. to take us to reception—we were going to the Old Bailey for some kind of court procedure. The sweatbox journey across London was long and nauseating, and on top of that, I was fretting about whether or not we'd see High Down again.

We spent no more than five minutes in the dock and the only memory I have of it was seeing Keith, the copper who had been arrested as part of the swoop on us. A big guy, former southern area amateur heavyweight boxing champion, he'd been Ben's best friend and Ben had been best man at his wedding. I was shocked when he suddenly burst into tears.

'I can't do this! I can't do it!'

While Ben gave him a hug and tried to calm him down, I just looked at him, probably with a face like thunder. I knew what this bloke was nicked for, and it was nothing compared to our problems. I didn't know whether to laugh or punch him in the throat. In the end, I just told him to be quiet. I didn't want our judge to be irritated at our very first appearance.

We made it back to High Down. Having ignored the bullshit advice from others at the Bailey—like one idiot telling us to strip naked and cover ourselves in our own shit so the security guards wouldn't be able to restrain us and throw us on the Belmarsh bus—we politely and simply asked the guards to help us out because all of our belongings were held in reception at High Down. The truth was we had fuck-all belongings—we'd only been locked up for a week—but the plan worked and that evening we were back in our old cell.

Less than a week later I was up early, around 6 a.m., when I heard the viewing hatch of our cell door open. A screw called out our names from a list.

'Pack your stuff—you're going to reception in 20 minutes. You're being transferred.'

'Transferred to another wing?' I asked.

'You're listed to go to Belmarsh.'

'No, guv, we were brought back here—we're meant to be here. We're not going to Belmarsh.'

'What's your name, fella?'

'Piers Ravenhill.'

'OK, listen, Ravenhill, you three will pack your stuff and be ready to move to reception in 20 minutes or we will wrap you up and carry you there while opening all the gates on the way with your heads. All your shit will stay here and you'll have nothing.'

Danny and Ben had been woken by the conversation, and when the screw had gone we all glanced at each other. No words spoken, none necessary. We got our things together and were ready to go. Mark joined us in reception and around three hours later—after a stop at HMP Feltham Young Offenders jail to collect a kid who made the journey even worse with his constant shouting and rocking the sweatbox from side to side—we arrived at Belmarsh in southeast London.

CHAPTER 9: WHAT MORE CAN I LOSE...?

I used to sum up what the first days and weeks in jail were like for me by saying, 'Imagine waking up one day in a foreign country with a completely different culture, a new and alien set of rules that were only explained to you when you unintentionally broke one and had to face the consequences; a country with a language you didn't speak.'

Going to prison was a very steep learning curve, but I was determined to learn fast. After biting my lip during my first strip search in Belmarsh, where I was first asked by three grinning screws if I had AIDS and had I ever been 'fucked up the arse,' and after being made to pull back my foreskin as part of the search then squat down naked over a mirror while they peered into my arsehole, I realised that I was being 'educated' from the minute I arrived there. The lesson was, 'This is Belmarsh. Enjoy the ride!'

From the first day of roughly 700 I spent there, it was a tough place with strict rules, severe punishments and a bunch of screws who were often what I'd call social misfits. In those days, they answered to nobody and what went on behind the walls of Her Majesty's 'flagship security prison' stayed behind those walls. Some of them loved it and took full advantage of the lack of accountability.

9MILLION:

The first six months in prison was about making the best of a bad situation both inside and outside of Belmarsh. Me and Ben worked our tickets and moved into a 'three-up' cell together, where we were generally pretty lucky with getting a half-decent third person. This was a big improvement on the cell share I had for the first few days, where I was put with a Jamaican on his second murder charge and another guy from London—a relative rookie on his first murder charge. They were easy enough to live with, but, when Akil the 'Yardie' pulled out a big prison shank to take to the exercise yard on my first day, I realised this was not what I needed in my life right then.

We also got jobs on our wing—Houseblock 3 (the induction wing, also known as 'Beirut' because of its justifiable reputation for volatility)—and we waited for the inevitable avalanche of damning evidence from the CPS. By the time the disclosure against me started arriving, the CPS had authorised a total of 52 charges against me and six other co-accused—26 of those charges were laid against me specifically. With plenty of thinking time, I'd already decided my only viable option was an exercise in damage limitation. I knew I was going to plead guilty for two big reasons: I didn't want a 25-year sentence and I knew there was zero chance of beating any of it. They had me bang to rights, cornered and on the ropes. My only target was the smallest huge sentence possible!

Within a couple of months of arriving at Belmarsh, the CPS was sending me cardboard boxes with hundreds of A4 sheets of 'disclosure.' Screws would turn up at our door with piles of boxes I had to sign for. I remember one day reading a few pages; seeing it in black and white was disturbing. I didn't recognise the man they were talking about—it might as well have been the case against Jack the Ripper. It was a shocking read, one I felt I could do without, so very quickly I would receive the next heavy box, sign for it and dump it straight in the bin out on the landing.

Danny and Mark had both applied for bail within a few days of our arrest. Being workers and having our door unlocked much of the time, I was able to help Danny by calling his family for progress reports. One afternoon, I felt very happy to be able to run to his cell, bang on his door and tell him he was getting out. We didn't see him again for about four months.

Mark was bailed a week or so later, and my enduring memory of it is that he didn't bother to come and say goodbye to me and Ben. He just left without a word. After that, I saw him once at the Old Bailey, about 16 months later, and that was it for a further six years or so. The only time I heard from him while I was in closed prison was when he wrote to me asking for a handout—I told him to fuck off. At the start of our time inside I'd had some niggling doubts about his ability and willingness to resist taking a deal with NCS, to take his punishment on the chin. Now that he had bail and hadn't had the decency to at least say farewell to me (we'd been friends since we were 16) those suspicions were heightened.

Six months into the chaos, me and Ben were well established on Beirut—we'd made Belmarsh probably as good as we could have had it. Top dogs on the wing servery, our cell door left open so we could make phone calls and use the (admittedly filthy and barely working) showers. It certainly could have been worse. Finally, we had a date—in September 2003—for entering pleas at the Bailey.

Around a month before this latest court appearance (I eventually had to be produced every six weeks for 18 months), I was called to the wing office, known as the 'bubble,' on a Saturday morning. I knew when I walked in something was wrong—the wing's principal officer was waiting accompanied by a vicar from the prison chaplaincy. When they asked me to sit down I carried on standing because I wasn't a man to make myself comfortable in their space and be whispered about as a 'screw boy' by other inmates. The news was bad: my mum had been diagnosed with terminal brain cancer. I thanked them for telling me, went to my cell (I was now in a single) and smoked a couple of big joints.

I wasn't in the habit of smoking weed or taking anything else in jail but right then I didn't care about screws, dedicated search teams, drug tests or much else if I'm honest.

In September 2003, I was taken in cuffs and chains from Belmarsh to Grayshott, Surrey to see Mum being buried. This is not one of my favourite memories. Most people there had no idea I was in prison and were shocked to see me attached to a 6ft 4in, 20-stone figure in a prison officer's uniform. I wasn't allowed any physical contact—not even a handshake —with anybody, although they did eventually allow me to have my six-year-old daughter on my lap during the service. She loved her nanny and she still loved her daddy, even though she now only saw me in the noisy and unwelcoming visits hall of my new home. Janine, still my girlfriend at that time, was also allowed to sit next to me; we were at the back of the church with nobody else allowed near.

I said nothing as Mum was laid to rest next to my dad, and, as soon as that was done, we left. I wasn't allowed to say more than a quick goodbye as I was marched away. I got back to the wing a few hours later, threw my suit into a bin on the landing and rolled a joint. A couple of days later, I pleaded guilty to 11 of the 26 charges against me after the CPS 'graciously' (but in reality knowing it wouldn't lessen my overall sentence) told my QC they would leave the rest 'on file' if I pleaded to the 11 serious counts. I didn't know it then, but I'd have to wait another 13 months to be sentenced. Danny was the only other person to plead guilty that day, meaning he was remanded back to jail and returned to Belmarsh with Ben and me.

Ben's mum died within a couple of months of mine. She'd been hospitalised during a particularly severe bout of Crohn's disease, and it seems all the weight loss during her stay finally led to a heart attack that she didn't recover from. I did my best to be there for him, and that was a time when we became even closer as friends. We were going through all this shit together and we had each other's backs, which was something special and would remain so over the coming few years.

Ben and I trained as 'Listeners' during those first few months in Belmarsh. Helped and supported by volunteer Samaritans, we first heard about the scheme from other guys desperately trying to be signed up in the belief that it would get them to open prison and day release in a heartbeat. I never bought into this idea. I just thought maybe I could help some inmates who were having a hard time for whatever reason. I think I was pretty decent at it, too, and I suppose the Samaritans thought so as well because it wasn't long before they asked me to become the scheme coordinator. I agreed to take the role and I was humbled by being asked. I ended up remaining a Listener and scheme coordinator in three jails over the next six years.

There are a few particular memories I have from my time as a Listener in Belmarsh. On one occasion, I got a call out to a man who I found hanging from the light fitting in his cell. He was a big guy but I held his legs and lifted him for probably two minutes—doesn't sound long but, trust me, it was long enough; this man was about 6ft 4in and 17 stone! I shouted and I shouted until, finally, a couple of screws came to investigate. One used his fish knife to cut the cord around the bloke's neck. He survived. I never needed any thanks for what I'd done but I can assure you that not one screw ever spoke to me about it—nothing.

Then there was the time Suzanne—the senior Samaritan and a lovely lady with a great heart—asked me as scheme coordinator if I would consider being Ian Huntley's personal Listener. Huntley, the vile murderer of Holly Wells and Jessica Chapman, was being held in isolation on 24-hour watch in Belmarsh after his failed suicide attempt while on remand in HMP Woodhill. He had to be dealt with in a specific way by Sams, and they decided I could be trusted to visit him, let him offload his troubles, without exacting revenge on behalf of those poor girls' loved ones and, let's be honest, 99% of the

British population. In a way, I felt honoured to be asked because this was a big deal. However, not only did I know that as soon as I got close to him I would have hurt him and then hurt him some more. I also didn't want to walk around Beirut with people saying, 'That's him, he's the Listener that hangs around with Ian Huntley.' So I politely declined.

I'm very glad I did. The man they asked after me—an older guy called Ian who was doing a 10 stretch for trying to sell military secrets to Russia (he was working for the MOD)—found himself plastered across the front of one of the tabloids within a couple of weeks, described as Huntley's 'best friend' or words to that effect. Everyone knew that some screw or other had given that story to the papers for probably the cost of a few pints of lager. That Listener's name, the list of his crimes, details of the passion he shared with Huntley for aeroplanes and even his photograph were all there for four million readers to soak up. That could easily have been me, and I'm very glad it wasn't. I'm not and never have been a 'friend' of any sex offender. In fact, during my time in Belmarsh, in the days when CCTV wasn't following us everywhere, I dished out one or two 'sentences' to various nonces the 'old-school' way.

The final enduring memory of Listeners is a meeting one day between myself, Suzanne and the prison's senior safer custody/suicide prevention officer. I knew this screw, and he was for the most part one of the better ones, though the competition wasn't exactly fierce. The three of us talked at length about self-harm and suicide, and I have to say the screw lost any respect I had for his supposed battle to save lives when he said to us, with a deadpan look and matter-of-fact delivery, 'Look, we want to prevent suicide and we're working hard on that because the paperwork's a nightmare.' I said nothing but I thought that was a disgrace. He made suicide all about the extra work it created for him, not the tragedy and possibly avoidable loss of life.

Another lasting memory... I was taken to the principal officer's office one day, apparently because they knew I had a grasp of Spanish and could speak it reasonably well. I was asked to speak to a 17-year-old Palestinian kid who'd been put in Belmarsh due to his allegedly disruptive behaviour in a Dover detention centre. I spoke to the lad and asked him to stay calm because basically this place would eat him alive if he caused problems. He was quiet but he understood me and I kept half an eye on him over the next few weeks and gave him extra food at mealtimes. Obviously lost and lonely—a boy in a man's jail who hadn't committed any crime as far as I knew—he wrote a note of apology on his cell wall one day and hanged himself.

That was very sad, but it made me angry, too, when I witnessed with my own eyes and ears the screws and even the number-one governor of the prison laughing and joking about it while they stood outside the cell even before the body had been removed. They called it gallows humour, something they needed to do the job they did in a tough prison. I called it being a bunch of disrespectful wankers.

*

As 2003 came to an end, I spent time thinking about what had happened that year. It had started well enough but I'd now lost my freedom, my house, my property, my mum—my life. I was making the best of it in Belmarsh, but I was in the routine now and I saw it for what it was: a place that applied extreme psychological pressure. It was like having my brain in a vice. Even the colour scheme was brown, the colour of the metaphorical shit we were all in! Our case was rumbling on in the snail-paced way that justice moves and I felt trapped in the limbo of not knowing my sentence. Every day I fried my brain wondering what it would be.

At this time I was also trying to work my ticket and land a job as a gym orderly. Eventually, and with the help of Jingles—a Jamaican friend recently sentenced to five years for dealing crack—I made it. I was over the moon. I've trained and kept myself fit my whole life and now I had broken the shackles of Houseblock 3, where one particularly nasty screw worked hard every day to block any wing workers from going to the gym. But now I was moving to Houseblock 4, where the gym screws wanted their gym orderlies housed.

Driven: dad trained as a Porsche mechanic before making it big in the used car game. We clashed always but I miss him.

Even though I was capable at school I had no interest in academia - I was all about my sport.

Scaitcliffe Prep School c.1982: I was quiet and shy even when I was collecting more sports trophies.

Hampton School; I look at this now and shake my head - I know how unhappy I was in my life back then

Mum & dad bought the Ship Hotel in Shepperton. An interest-free loan of £285k yielded £1.2 million profit after 3 years

Lost: evicted from here only weeks after my dad's death, my mum tried to commit suicide and was sectioned for a while

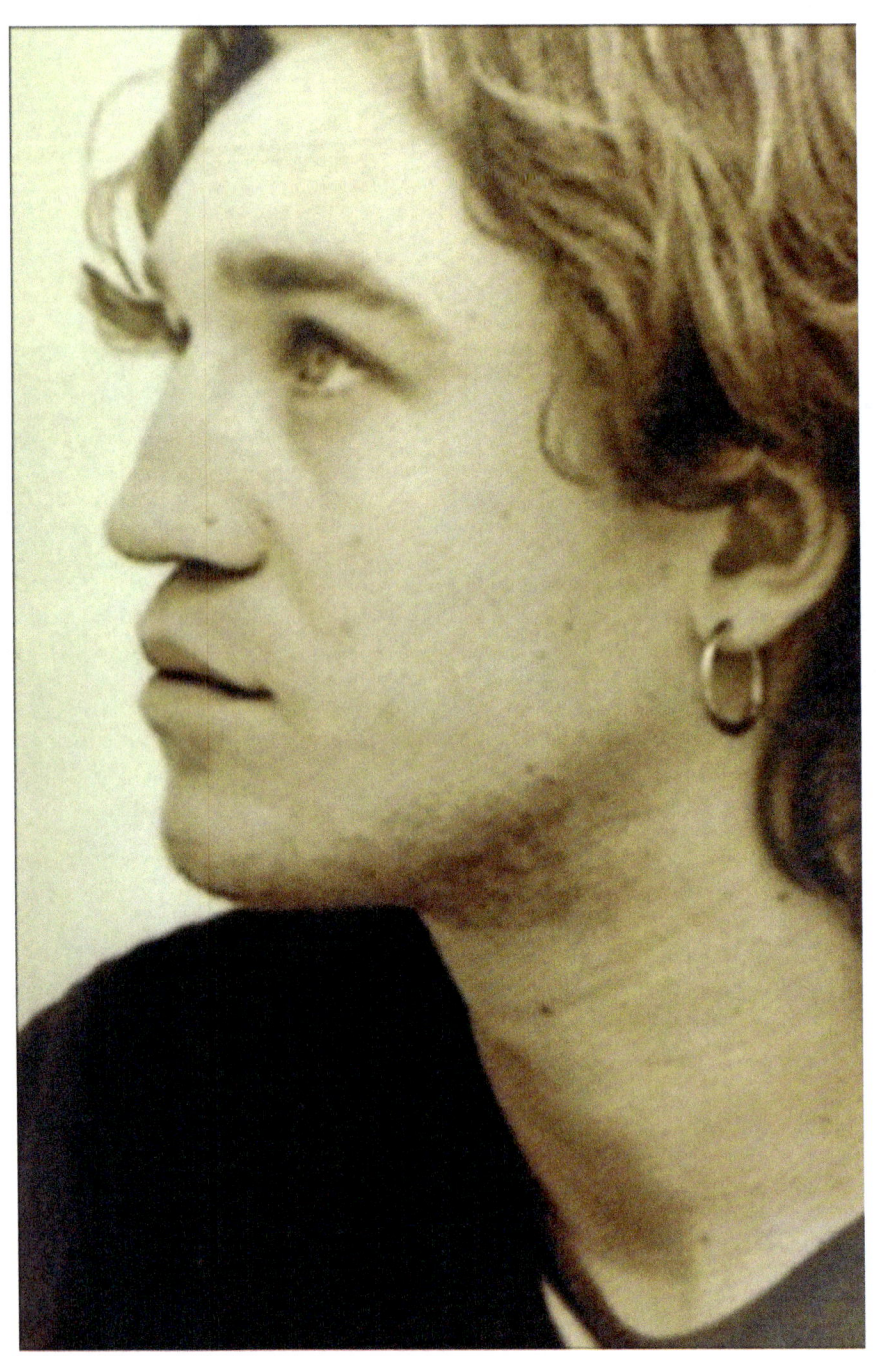

Looking up: aged around 22 and I was quietly but quickly - almost unnoticed - surging up the ladder in 'the game'

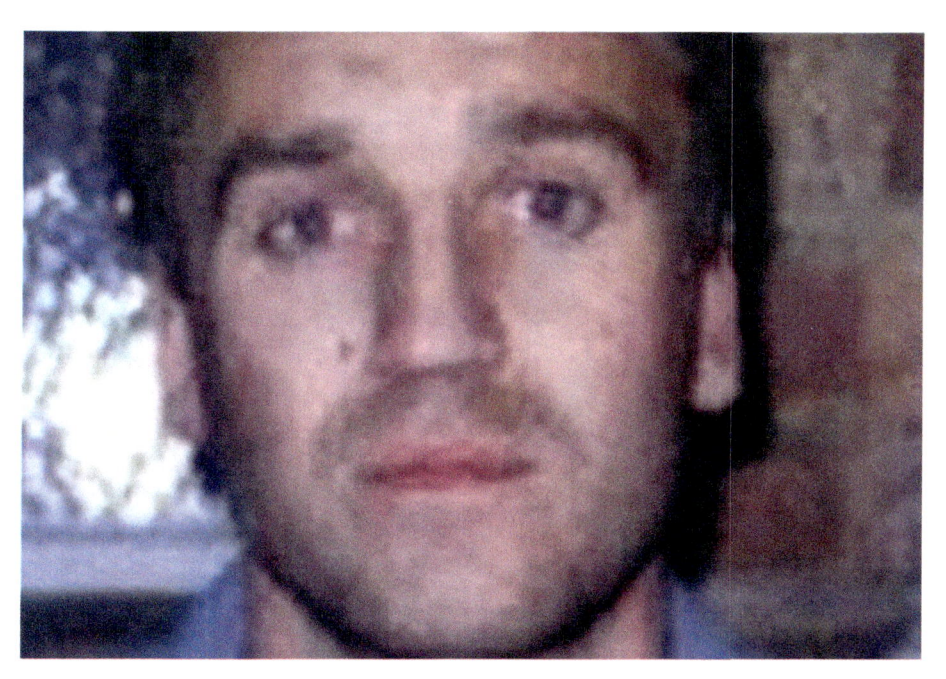

Arrest: photo taken by National Crime Squad outside the 'meet' Ben and I were nicked at by armed SO19 'stormtroopers'.

Confiscated: one of the many vehicles taken from me after arrest - my Porsche 911 complete with my private plate

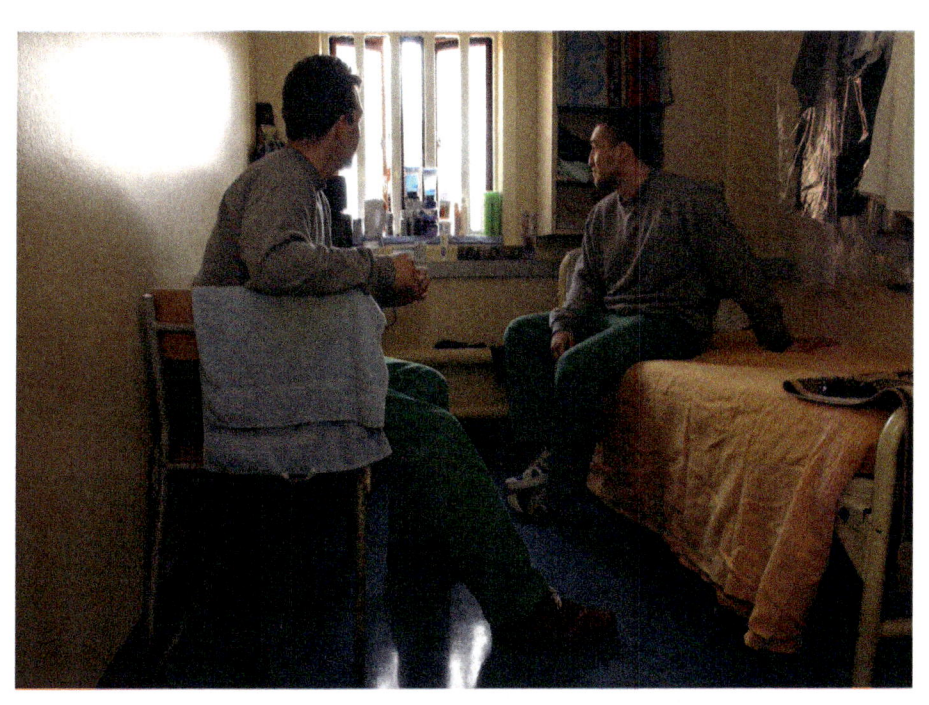

Me and Danny on 'Beirut' House Block 3 Belmarsh: Asked by a London daily news show what remand was really like.

Best mate & 'employee': No contact allowed with Danny since he left Belmarsh (2004). My license conditions end in 2031

Renaissance: the moment I surprised my daughter - then 13. My first day out of jail for over seven years

What is art?: a bit of fun near the end of my sentence... or signs that all was not well in my thoughts and attitudes?

CHAPTER 10: SENTENCING - THE NUMBERS GAME

Being a gym orderly was comfortably the best time I had in Belmarsh. Every day I could train and relieve stress; every day I had at least some time away from people and their noisy bullshit. The gym screws were very decent and, after nearly a year in southeast London, I felt as if I was being treated like a human being. I never had that feeling living on Beirut, and the fact that the screws on Houseblock 4 more or less treated everyone with the same contempt didn't matter any more because I was off the wing all day every day. I became the number-one gym orderly and eventually got Danny a job there, too, which was perfect because he was used to me being his 'boss'! We did our work well. As usual, I did more than my fair share, but I was happy to do so.

Finally, in September 2004, a year after my guilty pleas, we had a date for sentencing. Even this wasn't straightforward because Mark, determined to go to trial even though he was the only one with any shred of belief that he'd be acquitted, had a trial date set at a court date we all attended in August 2004 for February 2004. My QC, Grace Amakye, respectfully asked His Honour Judge Gerald Gordon to consider sentencing the rest of us—now having all pleaded guilty to all charges—before Mark's date. Judge Gordon agreed and we were produced in September, 18 months after our arrest.

The hearing lasted two days and it was hard work. The public gallery was overflowing, there were at least 15 coppers sitting next to the dock, occasionally giving us daggers, and I sat motionless as the CPS absolutely slaughtered me! When they'd finished, Grace stood up and made an effort—I have to say it was a weak one with lots of errors that left me unhappy with her work—to submit some form of potentially sentence-reducing mitigation, before finally came the coup de grace from, of all people, Ben's QC.

We had specifically instructed our legal representatives there would be absolutely none of the mud-slinging we'd seen with countless murder trials over 18 months that inevitably resulted in juries finding everyone on the stand guilty of murder, sometimes six or seven men all sentenced to life for the actions of one of them. Ben's counsel told him later that his job was never to help me in any way and he made a judgment call on his client's behalf. To be fair, Grace had disagreed with me when I told her, 'No words spoken about any of my co-defendants,' but I was savvy enough by then to remind her that she did technically 'work' for me and those were my clear instructions. She reluctantly kept her mud in her pocket.

After a morning in which I was officially ordered by the court to relinquish every asset I had, we were all called in after lunch for sentencing. Judge Gordon decided that me, Ben and Danny would be sentenced first and then have our sentences individually explained in detail *after* he'd completed that process with all the others.

'As far as you are concerned, Ravenhill, the overall sentence is one of 17 years. As far as you, [Ben], are concerned the overall sentence is one of 13 years and you, [Danny], one of five years. The three of you can sit down.'

I remember looking at Janine in the public gallery and the sympathetic, caring look she fixed me with, and I remember then asking Ben, 'What did you get?' because my ears had momentarily switched off when I'd heard '17.' Thirteen years was harsh in my opinion. I knew the level he was at, and he came out of Operation Sculpture with the biggest hit, I'd say. Danny was given a pretty standard sentence for the level of his involvement, but I've always felt bad for him because he'd only been working for me for a few weeks when everything went tits up. He went from plasterer to convict doing time in the blink of an eye

When Judge Gordon came back to me he stated I was the 'central figure' and I 'ran' the operation. He indicated it was only my basis of pleas that technically barred him from calling me an 'international drugs baron.'

'At your level, nobody was going to give you orders. The orders you received were from drug dealers.' The way he had constructed my sentence was very intelligent and well thought out. He made it all but impossible to appeal for a reduction, and when I did appeal a few months later I was told by the 'first' judge that, as the ringleader of a multi-million-pound drugs empire, I should consider myself very fortunate to have received only 17 years.

9MILLION:

My charges and sentences are complicated, but here are the main points of what NCS found and what I was given by Judge Gordon:

- 8.3 kg of cocaine, 100% purity in a diluted form (around 13 kg in total)
- 200,000 Ecstasy tablets
- 250 kg of cannabis resin
- further 'large quantities' of Ecstasy
- 73 kg of herbal cannabis
- another 114 kg of cannabis resin;
- 1.3 kg pure amphetamine;
- various stolen motorcars of high value
- loaded sawn-off shotgun
- loaded Brocock 9mm
- CS gas
- 50,000-volt stun gun

For each of the 11 charges I pleaded guilty to I was given—added up individually—a total of 38 years. Judge Gordon, I have to say, was as fair as he was intelligent. He gave me full credit for my pleas (which he didn't have to do because, as he pointed out during sentencing, a trial would have been an utterly pointless waste of time for me—pretty much 'Operation Certain Death') and constructed those 38 years in such a way that I had no cause for complaint. After 18 months inside, I'd done enough research and gained enough knowledge to predict my sentence would be 18-20 years after credit for pleas with a starting point of 30. It took him around

10 minutes to explain it all in detail, and I would imagine most people switched off after five.

Before we were taken down, Judge Gordon told NCS he'd considered their application for an official 'commendation' from the court, and it was denied. I've always wondered if the way they bullied Ben and made him pretty much fear for his life unless he got their proposed drug deal sorted with me surely played a part in Gordon's decision. He was as sharp as a tack, more than capable of working out what had actually gone on as opposed to the likely exercise in spin NCS had presented.

There they all were in their cheap suits sitting next to us in the dock—at least a dozen of them—and I looked across to see faces that perhaps said they wished they'd never been to Topshop that morning; no high fives that day. I didn't care either way really. I've never hated the police just for the sake of hating them, but one or two have done some things to me and my family over the years that... let's just say multiple crimes have been committed and I doubt that will shock anybody reading this whether you're a copper or civilian.

*

Back to Belmarsh and I guess we were today's big news. I managed to snatch a phone call in reception and was left heartbroken when my daughter, now aged seven, told me she'd seen me on TV and said, 'Daddy, I'm going to be 24 when you come home.' I explained the reality of sentences before she delivered the knockout question: 'Did you kill somebody, Daddy?'

I had to take a deep breath and gather myself before I could answer that one.

In the aftermath, there was now myself, Ben, Danny and two other Operation Sculpture 'persons of interest' in Belmarsh. Jason, who I knew from Ben's gym, was given I think four months for dealing steroids. He wasn't in Belmarsh for long—possibly a couple of weeks and then probably straight to open prison. Kevin, the now very *ex*-policeman, went straight on to the 'vulnerable prisoners' part of my wing and ended up with very little time to serve. He was never involved in what I was doing and I initially felt a bit sorry for him, until he took the stand at the Bailey and said some things in open court that, to my mind, made him a grass.

My hunch is that he agreed to do this for a lighter sentence. He never needed to take the stand—he'd pleaded guilty and was therefore entitled to keep his mouth shut—but he chose a different path. I wrote him a letter and sent it via internal post at the prison, and I didn't pull any punches. In short, I told him he'd have to live with the consequences of what he'd done for a long time. None of it affected me or my family, but that's not the point.

Finally knowing what I had to negotiate in the coming years was a relief. I remembered my QC, Grace, telling me she'd had a sentence of 20 years in her head. I remember holding my tongue when she told me not to bother appealing the 17 years and that in her opinion I'd been fortunate. I spoke to the gym screws and asked them to help if they could —try to get Ben and me a move to HMP Swaleside on the Isle of Sheppey in Kent. We'd already been told it would be there or the other security category-B jail, HMP Parkhurst, and neither of us fancied the Isle of Wight. I'd never have asked anybody to visit me if it involved getting a bloody ferry as well as making a long drive. They said they'd sort it for us. Now it was just a waiting game. I carried on working as did Danny until one day prison security turned up at the gym. Without saying anything, they put me in handcuffs and marched me back to the wing, chucked me into my cell and locked the door. I had no idea what to think until a couple of hours later when Danny shouted across to me from his window, 'Oi, mush, d'you know why they brought you back?'

'No, mate, nobody's said a fuckin' word to me! What the fuck's going on?'

Sitting alone I thought my nan, who was very ill at the time, must have died and they were maybe trying to find the chaplain.

'Mate, you and Ben have been made A-cat.'

I tried not to believe it but, when my door finally opened, all of my phone numbers had been blocked by security. I couldn't call anybody, and then, when the screws finally called me to the bubble to officially inform me, they explained: all phone numbers would need clearance from the Home Office. I'd have to submit on paper every last detail of everybody who intended to visit me, and they'd only be allowed into the jail after a home visit from their local police.

The next morning at around 6 a.m., my door flew open and there stood around half a dozen security and dedicated search team screws in their head-to-toe black outfits. I was marched to an empty cell on the other side of the wing, pushed in and locked away. Three hours later, they took me back to my cell, which had been dismantled with tools and turned upside down.

'Can you explain this?' I was asked.

'Yeah, mate, it's a T-shirt.'

'It's not on your property card, so we're confiscating it.'

'It's my fuckin' T-shirt. If it's not on my prop card go and ask reception why they can't do their job properly. Keep it anyway. If that's all you can come up with, you're welcome to it. Can I go to work now?'

'No, you can't.'

'Why?'

'You're cat-A now, mate. You can't work in the gym for security reasons.'

A couple of months later, somebody came to my door with a message from Ben on Beirut. Apparently, we were being moved to the 'unit,' which is a prison within a prison at Belmarsh. He'd been quietly told by a screw on his wing and wanted to let me know. That night I packed my stuff, which didn't take long since category A meant that, among a list of other restrictions, all my own clothes had been taken to reception and I could only wear HMP clobber.

My door opened at 8 a.m. the next morning and there stood Vaughany, my favourite gym screw.

'Wanna come to work Van Hilldonk?'

'Fuck off, Vaughany, they're putting me in the unit. I've been told.'

'Yeah, well, get your shit together because we got a call first thing. The Home Office have taken you off "the book." Let's go.'

That was a real moment for me in Belmarsh. I could now tell my daughter that I wouldn't be moved up north after all, and she'd be seeing me regularly wherever they eventually moved me to. No more moving cell every 28 days, no more three or four strip searches every day, no more having to wear their shit prison clothes!

CHAPTER 11: AS ONE DOOR CLOSES...

The days and weeks drifted away after we'd had 'our day' in court. One or two of the 'old school' villains around me gave their advice, which I appreciated while at the same time knowing I'd be doing my bit of bird my way and as usual in my life, I'd rise or fall treading my own path.

One man though... his words I never forgot. Paul was American, about 60, and had already served his 16-year sentence for a sophisticated Cocaine importation - all of it as a Category A prisoner. Since then he'd been back in Belmarsh - still 'on the book' as a Cat A - for over five years as he fought the US Government's attempts to extradite him home. If they succeeded, and deep down he knew they would in the end, he knew he'd never see daylight again. Paul said to me one day, "The road ahead of you looks impossibly long right now, I remember the feeling. Trust me when I tell you though, when you get to the end you'll think 'fuck me that went quick!' Take care though Piers... don't wish your life away."

Five months after I was sentenced, my cell door opened early one morning.

'Pack your things, Ravenhill. You're being moved.'

'Moved to where?'

9MILLION:

'Swaleside.'

This was the move I'd hoped for and the one the gym officers had been trying to help me with—a transfer to 'Stabside,' as it was called within the prison system. Now it was happening, the idea brought up all kinds of thoughts and feelings. As I rushed to find HMP plastic sacks and get all my belongings in order, I suddenly thought of Ben. Was he going too, or was I being optimistic in thinking my mate would be on the sweatbox?

Vaughany—PE Supervising Officer Vaughan—walked me to reception. Along the way, I thanked him for the job they'd given me over a year before. The gym had in many ways been my sanctuary, the only place in Belmarsh where I'd been treated much less like a number and more like a human being. All the staff were very decent with me, and I asked Vaughany to thank his wife for the many times she had sent him to work with a container of leftover dinner that gave me some respite from the daily gruel back on the wing.

Ben was the first person I saw as I entered reception. He was sitting happily, locked inside the big holding room and chatting to a couple of random blokes. I was happy to see him and knew we'd make this move together. In my view, everything we'd been through together over nearly two years made it almost our right to carry on marching forward as a team.

Me and my stuff were dealt with quickly by the reception screws, and it wasn't long before that holding room door slammed behind me. We waited to be called. And waited.

And waited. After maybe three hours, a screw came to the door and it was all systems go—except it wasn't.

'Bus is cancelled, boys. Grab your stuff. You're going back to your wings.'

If that wasn't disappointing enough, getting back to my wing was worse. My single cell was now occupied and when I asked the senior officer on the wing about another one, she laughed in my face before turning 180 degrees and walking off. Without saying a word to the two guys already in there, I dumped my bags into the three-up they'd shown me to before I was taken to work—to the gym. The news from there was encouraging. Apparently, a bus to Swaleside was coming for us the following day.

The next morning went well. I was walked back to reception but . . . no Ben. He wasn't far behind me, though, and within minutes we were again in that holding room waiting for the green light. It wasn't a long wait and soon we were handcuffed and slotted into our tiny individual cubicles on the sweatbox—which then broke down before we'd even left the prison! I sat with my head in my hands wondering if I'd ever get out of Belmarsh. But the breakdown wasn't what the driver had thought and, after a nervous 10 or 15 minutes, we were heading for Kent.

On the journey I thought about all the things I'd seen, heard and done in the time I'd spent there. It was all written in the journals I'd kept and I was determined, as I had been from day one, that when the time was right I'd write a book about my time there. From being humiliated by reception officers on arrival, to the countless trips to and from the Old

Bailey. From speaking to a bona fide serial killer, to beating up sex offenders while being the Listener scheme coordinator! All the screws that refused to let me have a five-minute call to my daughter when I came back from work every day—I knew I wouldn't miss those bastards. My nicking for 'endangering the health and safety' of an officer, holding a lump of a bloke up in the air after finding him hanging, being placed on 'closed' visits for no reason and having to say goodbye to my late mother while I was in chains and handcuffs. Being a category-A inmate and all the madness that went with it—all I could think was, 'Right or wrong, you did it your way, you survived and maybe even thrived in the end,' in a place where just surviving is pretty much a winning hand.

It was over now, and a new chapter of my sentence and time locked up was about to begin.

We'd taken it with a pinch of salt, but guys in Belmarsh told us there was carpet on the floor in Swaleside reception and the screws would offer us a cup of tea! I thought it was a wind-up, especially with the whole Stabside nickname in my head. We'd been told about that side of things and it seemed Swaleside was a place where violence was never too far away.

When we arrived, though, I had to smile. There *was* carpet in reception and a screw *did* make us a hot drink that he presented in proper mugs. I remember being spoken to like a human being. I could almost feel the weight coming off my shoulders within a couple of hours of arriving.

Not my best move then to nearly cock it all up on the first night. Put in a two-up together, Ben and me quickly had a visit from a guy we'd known in Belmarsh, and he came bearing gifts. A lump of skunk weed was put in my hand and that night I smoked a couple of small joints before going to sleep. The next morning I was called for two drug tests—one 'voluntary' that I hadn't volunteered for, and one mandatory that everybody got from time to time.

I was shocked. This was my first full day in Swaleside and the tests would mess everything up for me. I was lucky, though: I passed both tests. It's most likely because I'd had my first bit of weed for around 18 months and its trace probably wasn't in my system and coming out in my urine. Either way, I survived it and I kept my nose clean from then on. Over the years, I thought about what happened the day I smoked those joints. I was sharing a cell with Ben, but he wasn't asked to do a test. He also wasn't given any weed by our 'friend' from Belmarsh, and I wonder if I was in fact being set up by this 'friend.' It was either that or a bloody big coincidence.

CHAPTER 12: MAKING THE BEST OF IT

Having survived my little brush with trouble, I made a firm decision to knuckle down and live in Swaleside the same way I'd lived in Belmarsh, making the best of it. Unfortunately, my bumpy start on the Isle of Sheppey hadn't quite finished yet.

Within a week of arriving, I was attacked in the shower and somebody used a razor blade to cut my face above and below my left eye. I never found out who did it, but I do know it was a case of mistaken identity. As my attacker left the shower room and I tried to wipe blood and shower gel out of my eyes, he said, 'That's for Wanno!' I'd never been in Wandsworth prison. In typical HMP fashion, all the screws' attention was less on my injury and more on trying to find out who caused it. The truth was I couldn't possibly give them any information: I was covered in soap, couldn't open my eyes to see, and this guy was in and out in the blink of an eye. I made myself very clear to any screw that came to me, 'Even if I did know who did it, I wouldn't tell you lot in a million years. Go and look at my record. It'll say you won't get any aggro from me but it'll also say you can't put me on your list of wrong 'uns either!' They left me alone after that.

After a couple of weeks of sharing with Ben, we were both given single cells on the 'enhanced' side of the induction wing.

I moved into the place that would go on to be in my den for almost four years, and that's still the longest I have lived in one place since my dad's bankruptcy when I was 10 years old. Ben was given a coveted job attaching poster boards to cell walls around the prison while I became a peer tutor in education, helping to teach GCSE-level maths and English. Since I was in the education department every day anyway, I decided to do something for myself and ended up with a Level 3 City & Guilds adult learner supporter qualification plus a Level 3 Business Studies certificate. I abandoned a maths A-level course, telling myself, 'You're already battling this sentence and its effects, mate. There's no need for you to actively give yourself an even bigger headache!' I changed course, volunteered to be an unpaid 'Toe-by-Toe' mentor and started helping illiterate or semi-literate blokes learn to read and write English. For myself, I started some Open University studies that eventually led to French and Spanish diplomas.

Time moved on; Ben and I were settled. Back when we were there, every wing in Swaleside had a kitchen, and I took up the role of 'cook' for us. Nothing spectacular, a roast lamb here, a beef and vegetable stew there, but in time I added a few recipes to my repertoire, some from my Turkish friends, some from my Caribbean friends. I also taught myself to make ice cream, which in some ways was a bad idea because I started putting plenty of it away. The effects were balanced out though when, after around a year in education, I applied for a job in the gym and was taken on more or less straight away.

This, as it had been in Belmarsh, was a game-changer for me. After not very long in the job, I was officially (albeit against my wishes) the number-one gym orderly. I became a manual handling instructor, a heart start instructor, teaching guys how to give CPR, and I delivered all the gym inductions on Monday mornings to any new arrivals to the prison. I also gained some gym-based cleaning qualifications and became the prison's only A1 assessor for gym instructors.

When I look back now, I see two reasons why I did it all. I wanted to keep my mind busy and I wanted to show my family and friends—especially my now eight-year-old daughter—that I wasn't going to buckle. I was going to do my sentence my way. I added a couple of bits to the keep-my-mind-busy approach: reading and puzzling. I suppose the books I chose were obvious, but to me they were important. Among the scores of what I called 'classics' were *Crime and Punishment*, *Wuthering Heights*, *War and Peace*. I went through pretty much every Dickens novel and I also paid my dues by finally finishing my English literature homework from circa 1987. *Animal Farm*, *Of Mice and Men*, *1984*—all the books that, somehow, not bothering with hadn't derailed my GCSE!

CHAPTER 13: LOSING AND LISTENING

During my time in Swaleside, I lost both of my remaining grandparents. I took it on the chin when each application to attend funerals and say my last goodbyes was refused. Things like that... I'd decided long before that I would just put up with moments when the powers that be appeared to be making it personal. Deep down, I knew they weren't having a dig at me the man or me the inmate; it was much more that prison has a long list of day-to-day problems created directly by the, as I called it, Ministry of Bright Ideas.

I also had real headaches with the confiscation order dished out at the Old Bailey when I was given my 17 years. They started harassing me about so-called 'non-payment' in relation to the watches and jewellery the police had taken from my house during all the raids. It was complete madness. They suddenly told me I was expected to sell all my valuables —valuables that I hadn't possessed since the day of my arrest! Nobody had told me this at any stage, and I personally think they just made it up in the moment. How on earth was I meant to arrange and deal with the sale of items from within a high-security jail?

The confiscation unit backed me into a corner, so I had to get creative. I worked out a way to sell my valuables for a pittance, which the authorities agreed to, and I got the job done. It wasn't the end of the confiscation saga, but it got them off my back for a while, though they would be back with a vengeance in the years ahead.

As part of my knuckling-down approach to this part of my time away, I also continued to be a Listener, quickly becoming the scheme coordinator as I had been in Belmarsh. It was a real eye-opener. In 2005, Swaleside had around 85% of its inmates serving life for murder, and the numbers were rising. As a Listener, I saw just how many of the guys around me—plenty on every wing—had serious mental health troubles, and the number of times I found myself locked in the cell of the latest unpredictable, volatile and potentially dangerous caller was ridiculous.

Back then, a Listener would be on call for 24 hours at a time as part of the rota system; plenty of times I was woken at two or three in the morning to spend the next couple of hours letting people who should have been in secure hospitals offload their issues on to me. Luckily, I seemed to have the knack of helping people calm down and find potential solutions from their own thoughts, and I never found myself (literally) locked in a tiny room having to fight off an attack.

I learned a hell of a lot from the years listening in Swaleside, and I think I helped a lot of troubled souls. I might be a bit tired if I'd been out of my bed all night, but I was definitely happy to help my fellow inmates who were sometimes at breaking point.

The weeks, months and years ticked over, then one day it was suddenly Ben's turn to be moved on. He'd been downgraded to category-C status which meant, in theory at least, a more relaxed jail with a better regime and a bit more autonomy. In reality, though, as I'd find out when my time came, category-C jails are pretty much the same as category-B jails, just with more people I found it hard to like and screws who are in general much less helpful and much less inclined to be so.

The biggest thing about Swaleside was the screws and the governors clearly put an emphasis on keeping the day-to-day regime running like clockwork. No messing about with unlock times, movement to work, visits, canteen; it was very rarely interrupted during my time there. My theory is that their primary target was to avoid upsetting us lot because if it kicked off in a jail like that, regaining control would be very difficult. 'Keep them happy and we'll probably keep our teeth' was the impression I got. For the most part, it worked. It'll never be perfect in any prison, but, during my time there, major trouble was rare. Fair enough, my friend Joffy ended up with around 100 stitches on his arm and torso after challenging a newbie on our wing suspected of being a Peter thief (someone who steals from other peoples' cells), but personally, I had three fights in four years and my worst injury was a jarred wrist from punching one fella who had a very tough head!

Saying goodbye to Ben gave me very mixed emotions. We were so close after the time we'd done together and I knew I'd miss him, but at the same time, I was very happy to see him move closer to the exit door. It was now time for me to do a solo journey through the system and, after around four years locked up, I'd learned pretty much all I needed to know about how to quietly get on with it. I had friends around me who were ''stand-up' blokes—proper, decent, old-school villains—and I was generally well-liked by inmates and staff.

I took over keeping an eye out for a young lad called Chris, whose safety and ease of passage had become a mission for Ben and me. He arrived alone on our wing with a fresh 14-year sentence that wasn't as it seemed. Naïve and too trusting, he'd been paid chump change on a regular basis to collect bags of what he thought was cannabis from hotels around Brighton around once a fortnight. The police were on to his boss and grabbed Chris as he opened the latest hotel room door to collect another sports bag. The resulting sentence—huge for a lad of his age whose involvement was negligible—was for the kilos of cocaine he knew nothing about. He'd been royally fucked by the man at the top, had been promised a big 'drink' if he kept his mouth shut, which he did, and in the end, got a 14 and nothing from a bunch of empty promises.

I felt for him. Maybe he wasn't the sharpest tool in the box, but he was a decent lad with good morals and we became good mates. The only time I had to pull him on his behaviour was probably an example of how far I'd come in my prison 'education.'

'Chris,' I told him, 'you can either carry on sitting at this table and eating the meals I make us or you can carry on playing pool and snooker with screws, but you can't do both.' I didn't expect him to understand, and I explained to him that games and general 'socialising' with officers was encouraged by the Home Office as a way of gathering information through general chit-chat. I saw official paperwork on this at some point in my sentence and the idea was that people would give up intelligence—'intel'—without necessarily realising it.

We were both squeaky clean, but we also both knew plenty about the activities of friends and their friends, not just on our wing but around the jail. Chris decided he liked my cooking more than he liked pool!

CHAPTER 14: MAIDSTONE

Towards the end of my stay in Swaleside, I was sacked from the gym. On a Friday afternoon after going out to the prison's astroturf pitch for a game of football, I had a bit of a disagreement with Kevin, one of the gym screws. I'd known him for a while and I'd seen him acting 'drunk on power' dozens of times. He was generally a decent bloke, like all the gym screws were, but he had a real habit of blitzing people with verbal putdowns in a nasty way. Banter is banter, but Kevin let it cross the line into bullying. This particular afternoon was, for the first time ever, apparently my time.

I can't remember what he said, but he'd never attacked me before and I was so shocked that I instantly called him out. In front of some of the footballers and one or two of the other gym orderlies, I waited until he'd finished verbally belittling me. I looked him in the eye and spoke calmly and quietly.

'Kev, you now think you can ride me like you ride everyone else in this place. That's not happening, mate. But, if you really believe you can back yourself to do that, then let's go into the changing room, out of the way, and see if you come out on your own two feet. I'm telling you now, you fuckin' won't. Let's go and see if you are high enough up the food chain to treat me like a cunt!'

Kevin declined my invitation, and I left it at that. In the bigger picture, I genuinely didn't want to have to give him a hiding but I would have been impressed if he'd said, 'Let's go' when my offer was on the table. I knew he wouldn't take me on, not because I had a reputation for fighting but more because we both knew I'd hurt him. In that moment I could see it in his eyes—he had no bottle.

On the Monday morning, I went to work as usual and Nigel, the senior gym screw, asked me to come into his office. I walked in and there was Kevin, sitting down and drinking a coffee. Nige asked me if I'd like to apologise to Kevin and I refused.

'I've got nothing to apologise for, Nigel,' I said. 'He should be saying sorry to me. The uniform doesn't give him the right to talk to me like I'm a cunt, and we all know this isn't a one-off. You do it to everybody, Kev, and you know you do. You think you're being funny, but nobody else does.'

That decision sealed my fate and I knew it would. I knew I could have apologised and kept my job but my principles and probably a bit of misplaced pride stopped me. Plus, I knew screws have to back each other no matter what and wasn't surprised when Nigel said, 'Then I'm gonna have to let you go, mate.'

I shook his hand and left. I'd worked in the gym for a bit over three years but now it was time to move on. As it turned out, though, I trained *more* as a former orderly than when I worked there because all the gym screws let me in whenever I wanted. I don't remember speaking to Kevin again.

As it turned out, losing the job quickly became irrelevant. A slip of paper appeared under my cell door around a week later. It was a surprise. I'd never really thought about category C as the months and years came and went in Swaleside, but I was now deemed to be less of a security risk. At the same time, James, who worked with me in the gym and had made me a great meal for my 35th birthday, was also given his category C; we agreed we should try and move on together. I wanted to go to Coldingley, near Woking, mostly because it was the closest category-C jail to my family and friends and that would make their visits easier after years of traipsing from Surrey to the east coast of Kent. It didn't help my feelings when I spoke to a fella in Swaleside who told me about his wife and son having been killed in a car accident on their way to visit him in jail just before Christmas one year.

Lots of plans and ideas come to nothing in prison. James and I were put on a sweatbox to HMP Maidstone. We had one or two old friends there from Swaleside, and they gave us whatever help we needed to get ourselves on our feet in our new home. Our first request was for help to get us out of Kent wing, which was infested with mice and cockroaches. One night in the two-up we shared, I got up to pee. I had to switch the light on to find my way because the floor was an obstacle course of the bags we were living out of while we waited to move. I've never seen so many bugs! They were everywhere and I watched them scurry into the nooks and crannies while I stood at the toilet.

Our friends came good for us, and it was only a couple of weeks before we left the cesspit part of the jail. The new wing, much newer than the built-in-1819 Kent wing, was small, relatively clean and full of people we knew. Chris, who I'd kept an eye out for in Swaleside, was already settled there, along with half a dozen or so other old mates. This made settling easy, and there was a bonus—they got us jobs.

'Farms and gardens' is usually a kind of catchall job title for people in prison who work outside, sometimes moving items around the jail, sometimes cutting the grass or sweeping up rubbish. One thing I can say with certainty about the job: there were no farms and no gardens in Maidstone prison. My work was quite specific—I was in charge of making nesting boxes donated to local schools and charities. I didn't mind it at all, and I was never put under any pressure by our boss, Chris—a civilian prison worker, not a screw, he was a good guy, easygoing and good to work for. Soon after we joined his work team, he approached James and me with a 'business' proposition. Every Friday lunchtime he went out of the prison and headed to a petrol station with a few empty five-litre petrol cans to fill for our mowers and strimmers and he would return with all the cans filled with fuel—except one. One of the cans came back with five litres of cheap vodka in it. James and I would pay him £300 for that can. It was a lot of money but worthwhile. We would easily sell three of the five litres for £100 a litre, and every weekend we had a litre of vodka each to do what we wanted with. Most weeks, I would sell my vodka and keep the £100.

One time, though—Christmas Eve 2008 to be exact—I drank with a couple of friends and then carried on drinking in my single cell after bang-up. The mistake I made was accepting a small amount of MDMA—pure Ecstasy—in return for some booze. I know I took the drugs, and I know I drank maybe half a litre of vodka, but I remember nothing else of that night. I woke up naked on my cell floor and my head was banging! James and me had arranged to cook a proper Christmas dinner for 16 people that day... I let him down and took no part in any of it! It was the only time I ever took class-A drugs in jail.

Apart from the weekly vodka business, Chris did one really important thing for me. After six years locked up, I was still having big trouble with paying my confiscation order. The issue was the apartment I'd bought in northern Spain. I'd paid cash and owned it outright, but in Spain, I'd put it in my mum's name. When she died, under Spanish law I had to formally 'inherit' it before I was free to sell it and give the proceeds to the government coffers. This process went on for years, and I had no help from the confiscation vultures, who just told me to get on with it myself. This would have been quite a task in itself, but trying to do it alone, from prison and with the threat of an extra four years on my sentence if I didn't manage it was stressful, to say the least.

While in Maidstone, I'd finally managed to get to the point where all I needed to be able to push things forward was a passport for the Spanish legal people. I wrote to the governor of the prison, explained the situation and was told that under no circumstances would I be allowed to have passport photos taken for my application. Chris, bless him, said he'd do it all for me, including sneaking a camera into the prison for my photos. My passport arrived and was put in the prison's valuables safe until my daughter and her mum collected it for Gerald, my solicitor.

At the start of 2009, Maidstone became a jail for sex offenders and foreign nationals only. I was offered a move to HMP Coldingley, which I took without a moment's thought, and, after a few days, I made the move. Ben had been in Coldingley for a couple of years, and, in his letters to me, he'd said it was a decent prison.

Chris, my mate from Swaleside who'd been whacked with a 14-year sentence for the coke he knew nothing about, was on the same bus. By this time, I was officially a 'medical single' cell because of my ulcerative colitis, but I wasn't surprised when the screws asked me to accept a cell share until they could find me a single. For about three weeks it was me and Chris in a two-up cell on one of the shitty wings. I say shitty because at the time Coldingley was still refusing to put toilets in the cells on its four main wings. This meant that to use the toilet between bang-up at around 5:30 p.m. every day and unlock at around 8 a.m. the next morning, people had to press a button by the cell door and wait in an electronic queuing system. Sometimes it would take three or four hours for your door to automatically open. The rule was that, once you were let out, you had eight minutes to be back in your cell with the door closed and (automatically) locked. The next cell door in the queue could not open if one other door on the landing was unlocked. Probably 95% of people came out and stayed out for as long as they wanted, which meant some people who couldn't wait any longer had to piss in bottles.

Some even had to take a dump on a prison towel before throwing it out of their window. It was madness really.

As I write this in 2024, I've recently had to visit HMP Coldingley for work purposes, my job being to produce health and safety audits for the construction company finally brought in to install toilets and drainage in cells!

*After three visits to Coldingley - including giving a 'safety alert' talk about some unsafe work that had been carried out inside a deep excavation - I was banned from going there to do my job because of my criminal record. Rehabilitation courtesy of HMPPS!

CHAPTER 15: NO POINT IN WASTING OUR TIME...

We had to be patient, and I had some help from my new boss, the manager of the healthcare department. I was now the health promotion orderly in Coldingley and it was a good little job. I had my own little office (I even had a key for the door!) with a desk and a PC (on to which a previous user had loaded about 250 albums). I saw half a dozen guys a day and checked their blood pressure and heart rate; some had their BMI measured. I reported any concerns over these guys' overall health to my boss, and then the rest of the day was my own.

Tanya, the lady who had given me the job, heard about my inflammatory bowel disease and got me straight on to E wing, which was almost new and had toilets and showers in every cell. I had to share again for maybe a couple of months, but it was much cleaner and more comfortable plus nearly everybody on the wing was pretty sensible and what I'd call 'normal.' I heard other blokes on the wings that smelled of piss and shit telling their mates everyone on E wing was a grass or a nonce (sex offender), but frankly, I didn't give a toss what they thought.

For the first time since being incarcerated, I opened a 'shop' in my cell at Coldingley. Technically, this was not allowed as the prison service does not like anybody to be in debt. Debt in jail can cause all kinds of problems, beginning with threats and usually progressing rapidly to violence. I started small and never heard any complaints from the staff, so I expanded the business. Everybody in prison knows about 'double bubble' and all my punters were happy enough with my terms: a Mars Bar and a can of Pepsi... pay me two Mars Bars and two cans of Pepsi back on canteen day. I sold mostly biscuits, chocolate bars and cans of drink, which paid for my toiletries and food from the canteen every week. I didn't take the piss. I only did enough to make me maybe £20 a week, and I think that's probably one of the reasons the screws left me alone.

I definitely started to feel relaxed on E wing in Coldingley. I'd broken the back of the eight and a half years I had to serve and was edging ever closer to freedom. An issue popped up, though, an irritating and upsetting reminder that the authorities still had me in their sights. My ever-supportive solicitor Gerald told me the confiscation unit at the Old Bailey was now after my inheritance left to me by my nan—half of her house in Hampton. I had one or two heated discussions with the unit about my nan being robbed by them after a life of nothing but hard work and taxes but they stood firm. They told me to either sign and return the paperwork, or they would ask the court to activate the four-year 'default' sentence for non-payment of my order. When I thought about this turning my 17-year sentence into what would have effectively been a 25-year sentence of which I would serve 12-and-a-half years, I realised I'd been backed into a corner.

On New Year's Eve 2009, sitting alone in the dark after the cell doors were all locked for the night, I told myself, 'Piers, just give these bastards what they want.' They had me by the bollocks and I just wanted to finish my time and get fuck out of prison. I signed their papers and they went in the wing post box as soon as my door opened on 2010. Another £150,000 snatched... not from me but from my poor nan, may she rest in peace. It didn't help that I still had the issue of the flat in Spain to contend with.

My confiscation order was the reason I didn't bother going to my latest category review meeting in the spring of 2010. Everybody in the system knew that any person with an order that wasn't paid to the complete satisfaction of the authorities would never get their category-D status and would never see an open prison and all of its benefits, which included going out to work and spending time on home leave or on a town visit. However, I pretty much stopped thinking about that stuff and started thinking about the fact that it wouldn't be too long before I'd be released altogether.

A few days after my missed appointment, the wing's principal officer saw me on a landing and said, 'Mr Ravenhill, why didn't you come to your review last week?'

'No point wasting your or my time, guv,' I said. 'We both know I'm not getting my D cat—my confiscation order still isn't paid. It will be in the end, but I can't make it happen any faster.'

'I'm making you another appointment,' he replied. 'You might as well come along. I have to do it anyway, but let's have a chat about it.'

Over the years, it's been said to me it was probably a way of closing the shop down without any fuss. One or two close friends say the prison had suspicions about me and a female member of staff after we'd been seen talking, away from the crowds, fairly regularly for the past couple of months. Either way, when I walked into the principal officer's office, he didn't beat around the bush.

'Where d'you wanna go?' he said.

'What d'you mean?'

'I'm giving you your D cat. Where am I sending you to?'

'Are you serious?'

'I'm always serious. I've looked at your confiscation; everything's paid except this property in Spain. Are you going to give it up?'

'I've been trying to for seven years.'

'So… what bus am I putting you on?'

I'd definitely thought a few times about the 'what-ifs?' of my situation with the confiscation unit. I didn't need time to think it over.

'Standford Hill, please,' I said.

'OK, leave it with me.'

Yes, the shop was busy and one or two senior screws may have had a bee in their bonnet over it and what it was earning me. Yes, if there were conversations about the nature of my interactions with the aforementioned female officer, they were conversations worth having. We were having an affair, had been for a while, and the simple reason we weren't caught like so many others had been during my time inside was… I never told anybody. The fastest way to stitch yourself up in jail when you have any kind of coup going on is to tell just one of your mates. That's all it takes. Within a week half the prison and most of the enemy will know your business.

I saw it countless times, blokes being Johnny Big Potatoes; that kind of showboating is a security officer's wet dream. Put yourself on offer like that and they will take you down in a flash.

CHAPTER 16: OPEN PRISON CLOSED PRISON

I left for open prison three days after getting my category-D security status; the principal officer was true to his word and I was heading for HMP Standford Hill on the Isle of Sheppey in Kent. In a sense, I was going full circle because HMP Swaleside—where I'd been locked up for nearly four years of my sentence—was next door. However, in terms of the comfort of living and relative freedom, the two prisons were poles apart. I thought the screws in reception were taking the piss when they told me in a very matter-of-fact way, 'If you want to leave, we won't stop you. You can just walk out.'

They were being serious, though, and people did sometimes just disappear. But those who didn't come back from home leaves or town visits would eventually be found and returned to finish their sentence in a closed prison. Those who walked out of Standford Hill were also picked up eventually, but, because they had 'absconded from lawful imprisonment,' they'd also have to finish their sentence in closed prison before serving their new sentence for 'escaping.'

Chris, who had now been on the same wings as me in Swaleside, Maidstone and Coldingley, was already at Standford Hill when I got there. He came to reception as I was taken out of the sweatbox and handed me some paperwork.

'Fill that out now,' he said, 'and I'll run it up to Resettlement.'

'What is it?'

'It's all the information they need from you for Release on Temporary Licence. It takes them six weeks to sort out. The sooner you get it to them the sooner you'll be able to have time out of here.'

I saw lots of old faces as I exercised the freedom to walk around the entire prison unescorted. The atmosphere was tangibly different to a closed prison. I had help getting settled from one or two of these old faces, and the gym screws from Swaleside got me a job in the Standford Hill gym. Within days of arrival, I was a health promotion orderly/gym orderly —a job that I knew well and liked. Health Promotion had its own office next to the gym and we were pretty much free to train whenever we liked. I also became a qualified lifeguard; the jail had an indoor swimming pool and all gym orderlies had to be lifeguard trained for the small groups of elderly people and children with disabilities who had an open invitation to come and use the pool. I admired the prison for doing this and I was glad to help.

Six weeks after my arrival, I left the jail for my first home leave—two nights of freedom with a few rules to adhere to, albeit nothing too taxing. I'd thought about this moment for most of the seven years I'd been locked up. I had one specific plan and carried it out precisely with the help of my friends who took me from Kent to Surrey and my daughter's mum. I knocked on the locked back gate of their family home, and, as planned, my daughter was asked to open it and see who was there. The moment when she saw my face is one I'll never forget. She was six years old when I'd done my best to ruin our relationship; now she was 13, and she still loved her dad, the one who still worshipped her, still said she was the best thing to ever happen to him. I spent time with her alone (not being stared at by grumpy screws in chaotic visits halls), then with her half-siblings, both of whom I'd only ever seen in those same shitty visit halls. It was great... until later that day when I had to visit a friend and swallow some bad news.

It was a shock and it turned out to be a game-changer for me. The money I'd fought hard to recover from various people and places was gone—nearly all of it anyway. Before the apologies and excuses were over with, my mind was already racing. It wasn't a fortune, certainly not enough to retire on, but it wasn't an insignificant sum either. After being told how much there was, I silently left and went for a walk to get my head together. Twenty minutes later, I returned and said, 'What's done is done.' I asked for the remaining cash to be gathered up and brought to me, and with that in my hands, I left.

I can't say for sure it wouldn't have happened anyway at some point, but before I went back to prison I made a couple of calls to a couple of trusted associates from days gone by. By the time I was back inside, I was a drug dealer again. It wasn't what I'd wanted but it was this bad news and the rage I still felt about my 'stolen' inheritances that tipped the balance. For the first five or six years of my sentence, I was certain that

I was going to leave prison, put it all behind me and move on in my life as an ex-criminal. I have to hold my hands up now and say that could have happened, *should* have happened but it didn't and that was weak of me.

Things in open prison quickly deteriorated for me. I still worked in the gym, still worked in Health Promotion, but the transition from model prisoner to all-around pain in the arse was rapid and total. By the time I was handcuffed in my cell and marched to reception for a transfer back to closed prison, I was dealing cocaine outside of jail using a trusted delivery/collection man and the five mobile phones I had dotted around Standford Hill.

The raid on my cell—I had only myself to blame for that. I'd struck a deal with somebody in a trusted job who could collect large 'parcels' of contraband and deliver them directly to me. For a couple of months, I'd been flooding the place with all the things people wanted but couldn't get: phones, 'spice,' alcohol, steroids and even tubs of protein powder. It was a dumb thing to do. I was so close to the end and now my inability to keep my emotions in check was already costing me.

After around two hours locked in the 'cage' at reception, I was cuffed and walked to a large van with blacked-out windows. After a two-minute drive, I was whisked into reception at HMP Elmley and dumped into its holding room. I had 10 months of my sentence left to serve.

One of the gym screws unlocked the holding room door— I'd been in the prison for about 15 minutes and I had a job. Some of the gym staff knew me or had heard of me from my time in both Swaleside and Standford Hill: 'Come on, you're working for us now.' This was definitely the silver lining of a big cloud I'd brought to my life.

I lasted a couple of days at the gym before security at Elmley sacked me, probably because of the steroids I'd been selling in Standford Hill. The gym screws were good to me, though, and told me I'd be collected every day for 'work'; I just couldn't be officially a gym orderly. I didn't care about being paid for the job. Being able to train and not be locked in my cell for 23 hours a day suited me just fine.

I knew lots of people in the prison, some of them had been kicked out of Standford Hill for their own misdemeanours. I said hello to lots of faces I recognised from points of my prison journey but I mostly kept to myself.

CHAPTER 17: KNIFE POINT!

I spent around ten days in Elmley - most of that time in the gym taking advantage of the kindness of the gym screws who carried on picking me up from my cell every morning. I guess it didn't take long for security to cotton on. My door eventually flew open around 6 am one morning.

'Pack your things, Ravenhill!'

'What's happening?'

'Transfer, mate. You're going to Highpoint.'

Two or three hours later, the sweatbox reached HMP Chelmsford in Essex, and I was put in a holding cell in reception. Two hours after that, a screw put his head in the door.

'Ravenhill, there's been a change of plan. You'll be staying here.'

I spent that night in a cell on one of the wings. The only thing I remember about being in that jail was seeing the name Tony Adams carved into a brick on the wall outside reception. The former Arsenal and England centre-half had spent time in Chelmsford over his ongoing issues with drink-driving. The next morning I was woken early again and told to gather my belongings; apparently, my move to HMP Highpoint in Suffolk was back on.

9MILLION:

The sweatbox arrived at Highpoint at about 7 p.m. I was quickly processed and shown to a single cell on the induction wing. I spent some time writing down all the contact details of family and friends on the paperwork given to me so they could be approved by security and I'd be able to call people on the prison phones. My people were aware of my fall from grace in Standford Hill and subsequent 'ghosting' to Elmley, but nobody had heard from me for a couple of days and I wanted to give some reassurance.

On my first full day in my new home, I went straight to the wing office to hand in my list of contact details. When I returned to my cell, a big fella was standing in the doorway. The door was pulled to.

"Scuse me, mate,' I said and waited for him to move.

He looked at me, said nothing and stayed where he was. So I pushed past him, opened the door and saw another bloke inside. All my property had been emptied out of its bags onto the floor and the bed. I knew instantly what this was. These were a couple of Peter thieves. I didn't think, I just acted and punched the guy in front of me. I caught him in the windpipe with a clean shot and he hit the floor.

'Get up and get the fuck out my cell, you fucking rat!' I shouted at him as he clung to his throat.

As I started dragging him towards the door, his mate came in. He grabbed me from behind and there was a struggle that seemed to last for a minute but was probably only five seconds. I didn't have a clue that he'd cut me, but as soon as he disappeared I felt blood running down my face onto my white T-shirt.

I still had the other guy to deal with, and now I was angry. As he pushed past me, I grabbed the pen I'd been using the night before and—I'm not proud of this—rammed it into the top of his thigh as hard as I could. He disappeared, with my pen lodged in his leg. I had a four-inch gash down the left side of my face and now the blood was flowing. All this nonsense and I'd only been in the jail for about 14 hours! As for the theft—a pair of Prada sunglasses was their reward for a slashing and a stabbing.

About 20 minutes after this 'welcome,' the screws started locking people away again for the standard head count before movement—called 'freeflow' inside—for people with jobs to go to, healthcare appointments and so on. I tried to act casual when my viewing hatch opened to check I was inside my cell, and, even though I'd put on a clean T-shirt and washed all the claret off my face, the screw saw the cut.

I remained locked in my cell. About two hours later, the door opened to reveal a governor in the typical cheap suit and cheap shoes that seemed to be their stock management attire.

'Who did this to you?'

'I don't fucking know. Can you let me call my solicitor please, guv? Nobody knows where I am and people will be worried about me.'

'You won't be coming out of this cell any time soon, I'm afraid. Tell us who did this.'

'Listen,' I said, 'I've done coming up for eight years inside and you can go to reception and look at piles of paperwork with my name on it. If you find anything in there that tells you

I'm a grass come back and see me. For now, though, let me speak to my brief.'

The door closed and I didn't see that governor again. Eventually, a wing screw shoved a disclaimer under my door and told me if I wanted to make a call I'd need to sign the document, in which I agreed I would take no action against the prison for what had happened to me. I signed it, and about half an hour later I was allowed to call Gerald. He said he'd let my family know where I was and I felt happier.

I spent another seven days in Highpoint. On day six, I stopped the prison's residential governor as he strolled around the wing.

'How long is it going to take for my phone numbers to be cleared? I want to speak to my daughter. She'll be worried about her dad.'

'Your numbers will be cleared soon enough, Ravenhill, but for now, I'm more interested in who attacked you. Clearly what happened was some kind of follow-on from something that happened in another jail, and I want to know the details.'

I repeated what I'd said before about my record and what it said I was and wasn't.

That afternoon I was moved out of Highpoint—the risk of more violence had to be dealt with I suppose. Thankfully, the sweatbox journey was only about 15 minutes and we soon arrived at HMP Edmunds Hill, which was to be my last port of call before release.

CHAPTER 18: OUT OF THE FRYING PAN...

Edmunds Hill was a small jail with around 400 inmates when I was there. I went on to a decent wing and into a cell. I had about nine months left to serve and, although being booted out of open prison was a regret, this was in many ways the most comfortable part of my entire sentence. I found I could shrug off pretty much anything because I was almost at the finish line and nothing else mattered. The wing was relatively calm and I made friends with a few decent men there. One, in particular, was a Dutchman who would play a big part in my now inevitable full-time return to crime. For the time being I managed to get myself a mobile phone in Edmunds Hill and used it to make a few deals outside the four walls.

I was refused a job in the gym—unofficially I was told it was again due to the steroid sales in Standford Hill—so on a whim, I signed up for art class in the education department. This was a good choice—the class was quiet and there was only around half a dozen of us. It was pure coincidence but one of the other students was from Haslemere in Surrey, a small town I've lived in. Fergus was his name, and he explained it was his first time inside, serving around three years for supply of a drug I'd never heard of. Over the next few months, we became firm friends. A very intelligent young fella with Asperger's, which made him slightly quirky.

My time in Edmunds Hill passed quickly and smoothly. I had visits most weeks from my new girlfriend and her son, I could speak to my people outside on my mobile, and the screws left me alone until one day a few weeks before release. I was called to the wing office and told by the screws they had 'intelligence' saying I was bullying people and taking their Subutex from them. This was probably the most ridiculous accusation made against me in the entire eight-and-a-half years I served. I was never involved in Subutex or any other drug since my 'party in my cell and nobody's invited' MDMA cock-up in Maidstone three years earlier.

I decided there was an easy way to deal with it: 'This is bullshit, a complete work of fiction from somebody! The easy solution is I'm going to my cell now and I'll have all my stuff packed in half an hour then you can take me to the block (segregation unit). I've never even seen any Subutex—not once in eight years—but, if you think I'm bullying the junkies on the wing, put me in the chokey and it's dealt with.' The screws didn't like this idea and sent me away with a, 'We're just letting you know we're watching you,' to which I replied, 'Watch me all you want. Your informant is full of shit and you know it. If I were you, I'd get a refund on whatever you paid him!'

With just one week left, I was called into their office again and had the same conversation. I didn't start shouting or getting aggressive but I did remind them I had seven days left to serve: 'You can do what you fucking want with me. I'm going home in a week—you can't hurt me with this or any other bullshit.' For the record, I have never seen Subutex and have never robbed anyone in jail.

Finally, my confiscation proceedings came to an end. The flat in Spain was now realised, and, even though it sold for around a quarter of what I'd paid for it, this couldn't be held against me. I'd serve no extra time.

Finally, my release day came—16th September 2011. In fact, on the record, it said my release was on 19th September, but when they told me to get ready on the evening of the 15th, I kept it shut. Who wouldn't?

One last sweatbox trip back to Highpoint (at that time, there was no release from Edmunds Hill) but even that couldn't bother me. The reception at Highpoint was chaotic. It was a Friday and there were around 25 blokes being released. The holding room was noisy with fellas banging the door, and shouting, 'Fuckin' let us out! You're holding us illegally!' I sat quietly for about three hours, by which time there were around half a dozen of us left. One sat down next to me and asked me if I was getting out.

'Yeah.'
'And you've just sat here quietly the whole time?'
'Yeah.'
'Have you done long?'
'Yeah—eight-and-a-half years.'
'What the fuck? You should be going mad at these cunts!'
'Mate, listen,' I said, 'I've done a long time and there's one really important thing I've gained from it all—patience. It doesn't matter to me how long it takes these idiots to pull

their finger out: I'm going home today and that's a fact. I've waited nearly a decade, I can wait another hour or two.'

In the end, my name was called about 30 minutes later. I was given my discharge grant of around £46 and around £500 of my own money that I'd kept saved and then walked to the gate where my beautiful daughter and her mum stood waiting. I was calm and happy as we made the journey back to Surrey.

I'm ashamed to say I didn't stay for long at their house. I had an important meeting I needed to go to. That evening, I met an Albanian driver for the first and last time. I handed him a carrier bag containing about £35,000 in cash… and left with one kilogram of cocaine.

I was back in the game.

THANK YOU

Without the kindness and support of all these amazing people, this book would very likely not be in your hands today. It's been more than 20 years since I told myself, my family and my friends that I'd tell the story of my first rise and fall. Because of these people and their generous donations of time, money and unwavering support, here it is. And they are…

Cathy Aristidou, Sharon Austin, Karen Alpan, Tania Anderson, Olivia Barnes, Robbie Barrett, Kyle Baxter, Nita Brazier, Houyeme Butt, Evelyn Cairns, Claire Baldwin, Mrs Karen A Barnett, Alan Barrass, Pat Bell, Caroline Bickley, Bijsterbosch, Lynne Bissett, Fergus Blair, Karen Boak, Katie Brown, Donna Cade, Richard Cannon, Gemma Cargill, Derek Carson, Kim Cartwright, Chloe Collins, Sandra C de O Conroy, Kay Cornish, Maxine Corrigan, Darren Conlon, Anna Colquhoun, Sally Colquhoun, Sammi Craddock, Charise Cornell, May Crawford, Margaret Crossey, Louise Cunningham, Gary Curtis, Shelley Daley, Sarah Dalhousie, Elaine Dickinson, Linda Doel, Nicola Drewitt, D Edwards, Helen Edwards, Janet Edwards, Naomirose Elliot, Zoe Ellis, Dawn Embling, Lesley Evans, Kelayne Fannan, Marcus F, Layla Finch, Paula Gains (Hartley), Bernadette Gallacher, Tracy Gardener, Melissa Gates, Joanne Gayton, Jayne

9MILLION:

Gernon, Julie Gillespie, Lyndesy Gladdish, Beverley Good, Helen Goody, Caron Gould, Kerri Gregory, Lisa Groves, Sonia Hagri, Sandra Hall, Jackie Hambley Jones, Lisa Hardstaff, Carol Harris, Gail Harris, Jackie Harrison, Natasha Hathaway, Victoria Hawes, Wendy Hawke, Adam Hayman, Jacqueline Herring, Carey Hibbird, Lisa Hill, Toni Hill, Colin Hill, Alison Hillier, Angie Hodgins, Sharon Howell, Christine Irizarry-Amoruso, Gillian Maddocks, Malcolm Hoult, Ianelle Michelle Huggins, Kim Hughes, Linda Humphries, Sarah Irving, Sheona Jaworeck, Jackie Johnson, Hayley Johnson, Lisa Jones, Pam Jones, Mary Kane, Laura Keeping, Jodi Kent, Jackie Kennedy, Frances Kettle, Tracy Keyes, Donna Maria Law, Keleigh Law, Sharon Leask, Paula Lincoln, Shona Mackay, Deborah Mabbatt, Jillian Malcolmson-Hill, Polly Maples, Lesley Matthews, Vivienne Maton, Debbie Mcdevitt, Nikki McGowan, Geraldine McKenna, Louise McNally, Samantha Meares, Gillian Merrilees, Shaun Miles, Layla Miller, Ciara Murphy, Rosemarie Murrells, Catherine Nicholas, Rachel Oconnell, Caroline O'Donnell, Ian Old, June Okeeffe, Tracy O'Neill, Nicola Paine, Catherine Parkes, Angela Pawson, Judith Payton, Lisa Petto, Simon Pipe, Lorraine Piper, Lyn Poole, Simon Poole, Carol Popham, Carol Potter, Julie Powell, Zoe Powell, Clare Procter, Jackie Rice, Sarah-louise Reid, Lesley Roberts, Jacqueline Rogers, Maciej Rogozinski, Kelly Ross, Andy Rowe, Paul Russell, Tracy Ann Russell, Pippa Shaw, Penny Small, Angela Staff, Jackie Pownall, Sarah Selway, Jennifer Schofield, Joy Shipley, Toby Sillence, Linda Simons, Rebecca Smith, Jacqueline Solerno, Della Speight, Yvonne Spencer, Angela Staff, Antoinette

Starford, Dawn Stedman, Andrea Stevens-Hunt, Romey Strange, Philip Stuart, Geraldine Sudbury, James Sudbury, Sarah Sudbury, Ann Rich, Jo Telford, Joanne Thomas, Shelley Thorpe, Angela Timms, Lisa Tyers, Angela Upton, Alex Way, Sue Walford, Tim Walker, Mrs Watson, Alison Williams, Terrie Williams, Gillian Walker, Victoria Wareham, Sallie Warrington, Andrew Wells, Amber West, Jacqueline White, Donna Wragg, Carol Wilde, Elaine Wilson, Ellie Wood, Nicky Younger, Gillian Zebedee

Philip Stuart, Louise McNally, Sarah Dalhousie, Kyle Baxter, Julie Gillespie, Sharon Howell, Hayley Johnson, Keleigh Law, Simon Poole, Naomirose Elliot.

Printed in Great Britain
by Amazon